BIRD WATCHING IN EAST YORKSHIRE, THE HUMBER AND TEESMOUTH

by

Stephen C. Elliott

Foreword by Michael Clegg

Photography by Richard Fuller

With additional photographs by Ian Newton

Drawings by Richard George

With additional drawings by Robert Fuller,
Mike Morter and Catherine Elliott

HUTTON PRESS

1989

Published by the Hutton Press Ltd.
130 Canada Drive, Cherry Burton, Beverley
East Yorkshire HU17 7SB

Copyright © 1989

No part of this book may be reproduced, stored in a retrieval system or transmitted in any form, or by any means electronic, mechanical, photocopying, recording or otherwise without the prior permission of the Publisher and the Copyright holders.

Printed and Bound by
Clifford Ward & Co. (Bridlington) Ltd.
55 West Street, Bridlington, East Yorkshire
YO15 3DZ

ISBN 0 907033 79 2

*To
Catherine and Christopher*

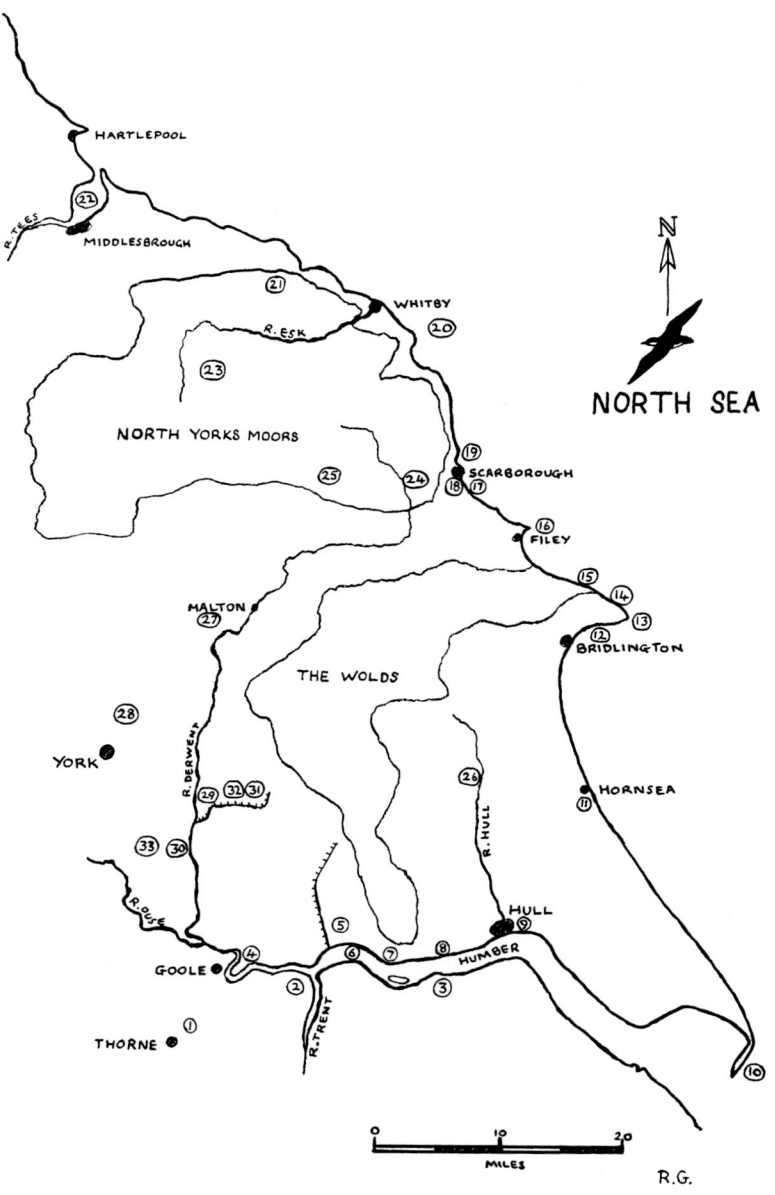

LIST OF CONTENTS

	Page
Foreword, by Michael Clegg	6
Introduction	7
The Humber	10
Spurn to the North Yorks Coast	18
Teesmouth	36
Inland sites	42
Other places of interest	60
Systematic list of birds (species)	65
Clubs and Societies	106
Further reading	112
Check list of birds sighted	113
Index	117

FOREWORD

Quite a lot of water has flowed under the Humber Bridge since I first met Stephen Elliott but you can be sure of one thing — wherever birdwatchers gather he will be there. Just a few weeks ago I was at Spurn Point with a party of birdwatchers, joining the massed ranks assembled to see an Isabelline Shrike — a lifer for me, and there was Steve sharing the twitch with the crowd of experts, beginners and novices as ever.

Birdwatching used to be by and large a solitary pursuit, but these days interest in birds has grown so much that it is now a mass participation hobby, pastime or even in some cases an obsession. And why not? It has so much to offer at all levels. But one thing every birdwatcher needs is information and when this is accompanied by some real help so much the better. Stephen Elliott is one who is always willing to share his expertise — and a lot of us have benefitted from it.

Now he has gone even further by producing a book on birdwatching in East Yorkshire which is going to be a very useful guide for all of us. And it is the real East Yorkshire too — not just the mangled remains of local government reform. And another thing you can depend on — this is not "stringy gen". Whether untangling the intricacies of Teesmouth or offering suggestions for good sea-watching the book is as helpful as it can be — like Steve Elliott in fact.

Michael Clegg

INTRODUCTION

*Come by the hills to the land where fancy is free,
And stand where the hills meet the sky and the lochs meet
   the sea.
Where the water runs clear, and the bracken is gold in
   the sun,
And there cares of tomorrow can wait 'till this day is done.
[Dominic Beehen]*

During the past few years there has been a growing interest in the countryside and our environment. This has arisen partly from an awakening to the fact that our planet is not a renewable commodity; that many of the changes that have taken place are irreversible; that many of our resources are drying up, and that once a habitat has been despoiled by the bulldozer or the plough, we lose part of our natural heritage. We are a dominant species, and have designed our surroundings to suit our own needs. In many respects nature has fitted in well with our actions, and the changes that man has made to our islands have indeed created a much richer and more diverse habitat than existed before the coming of man.

Our environment nevertheless, is a fragile balance of interrelated organisms and conditions. It is all too easy to upset the relationships between the individual components by accidental pollution, wanton discharges, thoughtless neglect, and deliberate destruction.

All of these situations greet us periodically. We meet them in the media when we see pictures of polluted beaches, dying seals, and poisoned waterways; and, as a result of our own experiences, of changes to our town, or when our village pond is drained, and of the lost hedges down the lanes we walked in our youth. These have aroused in many of us a need to do something to arrest further changes, to protect what is left, and where possible to create new areas that will allow man and wildlife to co-exist. Another factor that has developed in recent years is the use of our countryside for leisure. The pressures of modern life can often be eased by a short period of relaxation in the country. This helps to clear our minds and to blow away the cobwebs of cluttered thought that grow during the working week, and refresh us for a new period of activity. Ironically this new interest has led to increased pressures on some areas. Footpath erosion has become extensive in some areas, such as on the Lyke Wake walk and at Filey Brigg. More and more people want to open up flooded gravel pits and lakes to boating and water ski-ing. Birdwatchers themselves have not been entirely without criticism when a rare bird has occurred at a sensitive site. All of these activities are likely to increase in the future, creating further pressures, and in the end it is always the wildlife that suffers.

This new interest in our environment has led many ordinary people to join local and national bodies that are dedicated to the restoration of neglected sites, conservation of existing areas of importance, and the purchase of new ones. There have been dramatic increases in membership of many organisations such as the Royal Society for the Protection of Birds, the Woodland Trust, Greenpeace, and the County Trusts for Nature Conservation. This has given them much greater funding to purchase land, and volunteer working parties have kept management costs to a minimum. Unfortunately there have also been significant inflationary changes that have bitten hard into the purchasing power of these charities, so land can only be obtained after a great deal of fund raising. In our own area there are several conservation organisations that I would urge the reader to join or support; you will find further details towards the end of this book.

Of all the aspects of nature study, the interest in birds, and birdwatching has grown most rapidly. But why does birdwatching in particular have such an attraction to so many of us? This is so personal and individual a question that we have to look within ourselves and the points outlined above to find an answer. Birds represent the unexpected and the unpredictable. They change with the seasons, they are not always there when we expect them to be, they return each season like an old friend, and in lots of ways they represent the hallmarks of so many human characteristics. But most of all they seem to personify the desire for complete and utter freedom that burns within many of us.

Of those of you who are regular birdwatchers, to lots of you I am sure that these words will ring true; but equally well there will be valid arguments that many other readers could cite. Birds of prey enthrall many with the majesty of their flight, whilst the armchair birdwatcher often responds to the frailty of our songbirds. Many birdwatchers nowadays will travel long distances in quest of a bird they have not seen before, and gain much of their pleasure this way; this is called twitching. But whatever our motives, birds are gaining the benefit of increased protection as a result of our interest in them. Those of you who have only just gained an interest in birds will soon find that you have acquired an interest that is consuming, and helps to place us within the scheme of things.

In this book, I have tried to cover the places where you will find it easiest to pursue your hobby, and to give you a flavour of the locality with a sample of what you are likely to encounter there. The account is not meant to be complete in any way; indeed much of the pleasure of birdwatching lies in the discovery of something unexpected. If you should see something out of the ordinary on a trip out, then tell others. If it gave you pleasure, then it will do much the same for them too. If you are in doubt about the rights of access to any site, then please ask the landowner first. Most sites however have unrestricted access or clearly delineated rights of way.

Lastly I should like to thank Vera, my mother, for showing me my first kingfisher by the stream that ran past our cottage in North Wales when I was a boy. My thanks also go out to Michael Clegg for writing the foreword to this book, and providing many an entertaining moment whilst in his company. Finally I must thank my wife Glen for her patience, and tolerance of my hobby.

Good birdwatching!

The Humber Estuary

*Methinks I see a host of craft with their sails turned to
  the lee,
As down the Humber they set sail, bound for the northern sea.
Methinks I see at each tall mast a crew with hearts so brave
Going to earn their daily bread upon the restless wave.
[Three score and ten. Traditional]*

The Humber carries the waters of the Trent, Ouse, Derwent, Aire and Calder to the sea. It is a major estuary with little of the blanket development that has encircled Teesmouth. There are industries along the Humber of course, and many dump potentially toxic waste into it. If this were to increase, it could influence the number of birds that feed along the estuary considerably, although it is fair to say that efforts are being made by all parties to minimize it, as this vast expanse holds internationally important numbers of waders. Heavy metal pollution from industrial discharges together with P.C.B.s are finding their way into the food chain. There is little doubt that these chemicals are beginning to become concentrated in parts of the food chain, and although the Humber is still a relatively clean river, there is no room for complacency. We are at the top of the chain, and levels of these poisons that are being found in fish, and seals today, could be found in us in the future.

Many species of birds use river systems as a migration route to their breeding grounds, and the Humber is no exception to this, as birds can be seen passing along the upper reaches of the tributaries of the Humber in spring and autumn every year. Up stream we find extensive reedbeds of Blacktoft Sands, and there are the docks at Goole. Further down we pass Whitton Sands, Barton on Humber lagoons by the Humber Bridge, Hull Docks, and then on to Stone Creek and the mud of Patrington Haven. There are many other little creeks and reedbeds along the way, but the reader should discover these for his/herself. Eventually we come to the birdwatching jewel of Humberside: Spurn Point. Here the river widens out to release its cargo of silt and debris into the North Sea. It has carried material down from the Vale of York, the Yorkshire Dales, and from as far as the Potteries. This rich soup settles out as the estuary widens and the flow of the river slows, to provide food for the millions of bivalve molluscs and polychaete worms that live in the estuary mud. They in turn are a meal for the birds that spend part of their year with us along the shore.

At low tide the mud flats are the feeding grounds for thousands of wading birds during the winter, and during migration in spring, and autumn. Thousands of knot, dunlin and oystercatchers probe the mud for these invertebrates together with smaller numbers of redshank, curlew, grey plover and other birds of passage. Brent Geese also winter in small numbers along the Humber estuary; they are one of our rarest geese, and are given protected status here during their winter visit.

Thorne Moors and the adjoining lands   (Map Ref: 1).

Although this vast expanse is on the limit of our geographical area it extends towards Goolefields and is a quite remarkable habitat. There are little signs now of any cultivation, as most of it has grown over with silver birch and bracken; however there are the remains of old peat excavations. Some parts of Thorne Moors are being spoiled by local people who are digging up more, and wider areas of the peat. Some of the ancient diggings which have become flooded and well colonized provide a home for mallard and black-headed gulls to breed. It is a difficult place to enter as the ground is undulating, and dense with vegetation. However there are several well defined trails which are quite easy to follow. Redpolls occur there in large numbers, and in summer, whinchat, redstart, green woodpecker, great spotted woodpecker, nightjar and woodcock also occur regularly and may be at least heard, even if they are not seen. This is also a place where hobby occurs most years, and this most agile and graceful raptor finds plenty of food from the large insect population, and the hirundines there. The fields towards Goole are a good place to look out for dotterel in springtime. They stop here each year in mid May, and are in fine breeding plumage as they head for the Scottish Highlands. A flock of 60 birds was seen in 1987. Hatfield Carrs is where quail often are heard in springtime, but they are very difficult to observe, and can cover large distances by simply running through the grass ahead of any potential observer.

In the winter there is a hen harrier roost, and rough-legged buzzard are sometimes reported. One winter they were joined by a massive visitor for a day, a sea eagle.

Blacktoft Sands   (Map Ref: 2).

This is an enormous expanse of natural reedbed at the confluence of the Ouse and the Trent, and it is managed by the RSPB who employ a full time warden. There is an information centre there and a notice board to let you know what has been seen that day. In recent years some of the reedbed has been scraped away to create open water for wildfowl, and to make muddy areas for waders to rest or feed at high tide. There are always good numbers of regular birds such as dunlin, redshank etc., and on passage ruff, green sandpipers, little stints, curlew sandpipers, and greenshank occur. There are 6 hides along the edge of the reserve, and from these some excellent views of marsh harrier, hen harrier, and short-eared owl can be seen. Some very rare vagrants have turned up at Blacktoft such as penduline tit, Hudsonian godwit, and red-necked stint, the latter two constituting the first recorded occurrences in the UK. This reserve is also one of the best places to see bearded reedlings, with over 500 having been recorded in the autumn.

There are regular guided tours of the reserve at weekends to look for birds of the season: e.g. waders in autumn, spring migrants, the dawn chorus, or the winter hen harrier roost. There is a small charge for the tour, and binoculars may be hired for the trip. At the end of the visit hot soup and bacon butties are usually provided to ward off the hunger pangs! Further details may be obtained from the reserve warden. Entry is free to RSPB members, and a small charge is made to non-members. Volunteer wardens are taken on regularly and help to improve habitats, maintain hides etc., as well as to do useful daily jobs such as wader counts, and to run the visitor centre.

Barton on Humber   (Map Ref: 3).

There is a string of lagoons here that are the remains of old clay workings, that runs east to west of the Humber Bridge on the south bank. The lagoons are well fringed with reeds, and bearded reedlings breed here in small numbers. They may be viewed from the public hides there, or from the Humber embankment which marks the start of the Viking Way. The Viking Way is a 140 mile long-distance walk from here to Oakham. Mallard, teal, gadwall, shoveller and wigeon are regulars on the lagoons, and there is also a scrape which usually has a small number of waders feeding on it such as common sandpiper, ringed plover and dunlin. Scarcer waders also turn up here from time to time, such as little stints, and curlew sandpipers.

The lagoons extend to New Holland, where there is another hide looking out over the estuary. This is a good spot to see sea duck such as scaup and pintail, and of course there are always waders along the edge of the river to be seen such as turnstone and oystercatchers. Cormorants fish all along the estuary, and occasionally red-throated divers may be seen.

There is an information centre just to the east of the bridge which is open at weekends and holidays. Here you may buy their newsletter 'Waterside' which will tell you more about the area, and all about the latest management and conservation projects.

Saltmarsh Delft   (Map Ref: 4).

This is a small reserve managed by Yorkshire Wildlife Trust on the north of the Humber between the villages of Skelton and Saltmarsh. The reserve is fringed on the south and east by hawthorn and to the north by the main railway line to Hull. There is a public viewing hide which can be reached by a path running along the base of the embankment, although permission to walk along the path should be obtained from British Rail. The reserve is mainly reedbed with some open water and attracts wildfowl in small numbers in the winter, and reed warbler, sedge warblers, willow warbler and blackcap in the spring. There is open farmland around the reserve which holds corn buntings, cuckoo, and red legged partridge. The reserve had its glory year in 1984 when a great reed warbler spent a few

Corn bunting.

weeks there in the summer, and may also have been present in other years; bittern and bearded reedling have also been recorded there. A visit to this reserve would pleasantly fit in with a walk along the Humber embankment.

Market Weighton canal   (Map Ref: 5)

This stretch of canal is very under watched, and provides a lot of scope for any birdwatcher in the locality. The common bird census is conducted every year by the British Trust for Ornithology, and few reports come from areas such as this. It is free of reed margin at its lower reaches where it empties into the Humber just upstream from Whitton Sand, but there are phragmites reed beds in parts of the upper courses towards Market Weighton that have the usual summer complement of reed and sedge warblers. At the intersection with the Goole to Hull railway there is a string of ponds that would also deserve regular observance. So take up the challenge, you never know what you might find there!

Broomfleet Pools   (Map Ref: 6)

These are on private land near the village of Broomfleet on the north of the Humber, and permission must be obtained to visit them. It consists of two main lagoons, one of which is open and free of encroaching vegetation, except for a small reedbed, whilst the other is largely invaded by willow. There are feral greylag geese and great crested grebes there all year, but in the winter the numbers of geese rise and are joined by many ducks, and are sometimes joined by less common geese such as bean. Smew are also fond of this spot, and when most of the local water is iced over they become concentrated on any small open stretches that occur here. Male smew are always scarce, but here they seem to occur regularly in winter.

Humber Wildfowl Refuge   (Map Ref: 7)

This lies on the north bank of the Humber to the east of the village of Faxfleet. There are reedbeds which often have bearded reedlings, and two pools for wildfowl to shelter in at high tide. These pools are also used for breeding by tufted duck, mallard, and mute swan. Along the bank of the estuary there is a rough saltmarsh which often has short-eared owls and merlin in winter, and this is also a very good vantage point to see birds of prey across the river at Blacktoft Sands, where hen harriers in winter, and marsh harrier in summer, can be seen quartering the reed beds. Ringed plover breeds there, and jack snipe are sometimes flushed from the saltings in winter.

There is a lot of wildfowling all along the Humber on both banks, so don't be surprised to see people armed with shotguns.

Whitton Sand and Read's Island   (Map Ref: 7)

Whitton Sands is an island sand-bar in the Humber where shelduck, pintail, and pinkfeet can be seen in large numbers during the winter. Mallard, wigeon, and teal feed and roost around the edge, and in autumn large numbers of dunlin, redshank, oystercatchers congregate. Curlew sandpipers, black-tailed, and bar-tailed godwits turn up in smaller numbers. Flocks of snow buntings have been seen flying around there in winter; but you really need a telescope to get reasonable views of the birds, as the island is about a half kilometre into the river. A good place to see over to Whitton Sands is from where Market Weighton Canal empties into the estuary.

The south bank is a good place to look out to Read's Island, and similar birds can be seen around the edge (as at Whitton Sands), but as it has a good cover of rough grass, common ground birds can be seen there. It always surprises me to look out across the estuary and see pheasants and fallow deer grazing there.

Brough Haven   (Map Ref: 7)

This is a small tidal creek near the village of Brough on the north of the Humber. It attracts lots of redshank, dunlin, ringed plover, and curlew. Bar-tailed godwits and grey plovers can also be seen in autumn as well as the unexpected wader. There is a large mud bank that mallard and shelduck roost on at low water, along with many more waders. A pleasant walk may be taken down the footpath which runs along the shoreline towards the ponds at Welton Waters, and the estuary is always full of waders. There are a lot of Roman artefacts in this area, as this is where Roman troops could cross the Humber at low water on spring tides. Several people have tried to recreate this event, but most have ended up floundering in the mud feeling very cold!

Welton Waters   (Map Ref: 7)

There are two large lakes here that are very attractive to birds, and are capable of holding hundreds of ducks in autumn. Sadly there is a lot of disturbance as a great deal of shooting goes on, and there is a water ski club at one of them. Nevertheless cormorants, gadwall, wigeon, teal, mallard, tufted duck, and pochard can be found there, and goldeneye, goosander and grebes turn up in winter.

There are cuckoos, reed and sedge warblers in summer, and bearded reedlings have been recorded. The potential for this site for birdwatching is considerable, as it is underwatched, but still records scarce birds from time to time, such as woodchat shrike.

Humber Bridge Country Park [Little Switzerland] (Map Ref: 8).

The water is wide, I cannot cross o'er
Neither have I strong wings to fly.
Bring me a boat that can carry two,
And both shall row, my love and I.

Well there is no need to row there nowadays, since the Humber bridge was built to connect the lagoons at Barton on Humber on the south bank with Little Switzerland on the north of the river.

Humberside County Council have created a nature trail in woodland next to the bridge on the north bank. It is managed by their Country Ranger and many outside bodies have helped in the creation of the walkways. School parties are welcome here and are escorted by the ranger who will explain the importance of conservation, and tell children all about the wildlife there.

The park consists of the old Hessle chalk quarry and Little Switzerland. There are cliffs, open meadow, scrub, woodland, and open water. The water gets a few birds, such as moorhen and pied wagtail, but its main interest lies beneath the water in its newts and invertebrate life. The park gets a good complement of birds throughout the year with lots of warblers in the summer, and flocks of fieldfare and redwing in winter. Quite a lot of buddleia grows there, and in summer there is a good population of butterflies that drink nectar from its flowers, e.g. peacock and red admirals. The shore is always worth a look, as there are waders such as dunlin and redshank there at all times of the year, and wildfowl such as shelduck can be seen in flight along the river. There is an old 5 sailed windmill to see on the foreshore.

Hull Docks (Map Ref: 9).

Now you're up on deck, you're a fisherman,
You can swear and show a manly bearing,
Take your turn on watch with the other fellows,
Whilst you're searching for the shoals of herring.
[Shoals of herring - traditional]

You can get to the waterfront from the Hedon road out of Hull.

Then take the turn off towards the North Sea Ferry Terminal which will take you to a small car park. You may walk east or west along public footpaths which run along the water edge and although this may not be the prettiest of places to go to, the air is bracing, and there are always birds passing. Walking west will take you to where Holderness Drain enters the Humber. Gulls feed here at high tide, and black terns are seen regularly in spring and autumn. Walking further along will take you to the old Alexandra Dock, but many parts of the wharfe are extremely hazardous, so keep to the public rights of way. Glaucous, Iceland, and ring-billed gull have been recorded here by the regular watchers. In spring, broad-billed sandpiper, white stork, and black kite are among the unlikely birds that have been seen.

Spurn Point and the immediate area   (Map Ref: 10).

This 3 mile-long extension of Holderness has been under severe threat from the North Sea for several years, and it is only a matter of time before the sea cuts the peninsula in half and creates an island out of the Southernmost aspect where the coastguard station is at the moment. Ironically it is the sea that was responsible for the creation of Spurn, as for centuries erosion along the east coast of Yorkshire has resulted in the creation of several successive points such as the present one, only for further erosion to remove them, as is happening now.

Several million tons of boulder clay have been dumped along the seaward edge to try to keep back the tides, but this will only delay the inevitable as Spurn has been breached several times in recent years, despite heroic efforts to save it. The first breach destroyed Yorkshire's only site of Monkey orchid. This was a great loss, and there are other interesting plants such as yellow-wort, spiny restharrow, spring beauty which whilst they are not all that rare, nevertheless are under threat.

It is a very narrow peninsula, with extensive sea buckthorn. This is covered in orange berries in autumn which provide food for the many thousands of Scandinavian thrushes such as redwings, fieldfare, and blackbirds that migrate to this country each year.

Spurn seems to act as a funnel for birds migrating along the east coast in spring and autumn. Relatively common birds such as

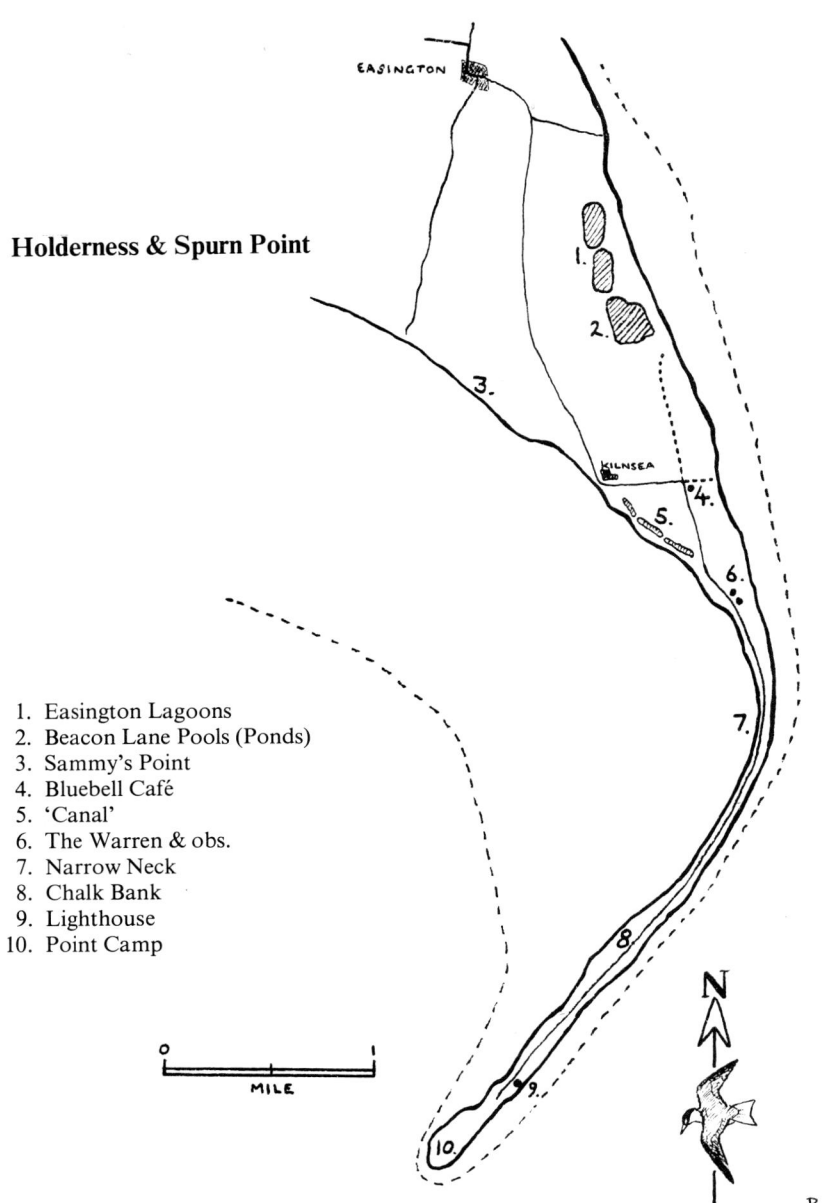

Holderness & Spurn Point

1. Easington Lagoons
2. Beacon Lane Pools (Ponds)
3. Sammy's Point
4. Bluebell Café
5. 'Canal'
6. The Warren & obs.
7. Narrow Neck
8. Chalk Bank
9. Lighthouse
10. Point Camp

redstarts, pied flycatchers, goldcrests, whimbrel, grey plovers etc., can be present in substantial numbers during migration. During fall conditions some quite remarkably rare birds can turn up! In recent years Radde's warbler, Pallas's warbler, subalpine warbler, thrush nightingale, red-rumped swallow, black kite, bee-eater, hoopoe, red-throated pipit, Richard's pipit, greater sand plover, and many more have been spotted!! For a more complete picture please refer to the annual report which can be obtained from the shop at the Warren, or by post from Yorkshire Wildlife Trust at York. The reserve is owned by the Trust and a full time warden is present throughout the year. There is an observatory where birdwatchers from all over the country come to stay. Some come just for the bird watching, whilst others attend the ringing courses held each year. There are several Heligoland traps which funnel the birds into an ever decreasing space until they are trapped in a small box, ringed, weighed, and measured, before being released. Mist nets are also used in some inaccessible areas to trap small birds as they pass along the point. These are very fine gossamer nets that cannot be seen by the birds, so they fly into them. They are removed from the net gently before they are processed in the observatory, and then released to continue their migration with a small band on their leg that will identify the bird should it be recovered in another country. Ringing studies help to plot migration routes and help to provide necessary evidence for the need to conserve areas that are important along the birds' migration routes.

There is a sea watching hide behind the observatory and skuas, divers, and migrating wildfowl such as teal and wigeon, can be seen moving along the coast from it. This is a popular spot in autumn and winter, but always go with an eye to the weather, as the wind coming off the sea is a lazy wind!

There are several areas that are popular with birdwatchers such as the Point which is an almost impenetrable tangle of sea buckthorn, and elder; but often attracts scarce birds on passage. The birds are not always easy to see there, but patience can often be rewarded with an icterine warbler, or a barred warbler, or a black redstart or...

At the Narrow Neck the sea and the estuary are only a few metres apart, and waders such as turnstones, curlew, oystercatchers and dunlin work their way along the tide line feeding there. At high tide the birds become more and more concentrated in numbers, and flocks containing many hundreds of birds move along the estuary.

Some roost at Chalk Bank until high tide, and this is a good place to look out for bar-tailed godwits and Sandwich terns as they rest until the tide turns.

The areas around the villages of Kilnsea and Easington
(Map Ref: 10).

These villages are to the north of Spurn, and like other villages in the past, the land to the east of them is under threat from the sea. The Bluebell cafe was built in 1847 at a distance of over 500yds from the sea. Today it stands a mere 80yds away from the water, and will no doubt one day feel the wash of the sea around its foundations. When you visit Spurn, you will find there are several spots that are always worth checking.

The Triangle is an area between the canal and the main road to Spurn. On the west side there is a canal cutting, fringed with reeds that have sedge warblers throughout the summer, and the gorse banks attract warblers in autumn and spring. They should be checked carefully as Savi's warbler and aquatic warbler have been seen there. The fields in the Triangle attract whimbrel, redshank, fieldfare, redwing, and many other small birds throughout the year. It is difficult to predict what may turn up here at migration time, as just about anything can be seen. In the past few years red-backed shrike, bluethroat, night heron, thrush nightingale, American golden plover, rock thrush, and possibly even oriental cuckoo, have been recorded. One of the most favoured places is the "big hedge" near the entrance to the reserve; it is thick with lots of surrounding undercover, and is "well worked" by the local birdwatchers.

Beacon Lane runs down to the sea from the cafe, and has an untidy line of tangled and stunted hawthorn bushes along it. These again are always worth looking at as they are one of the first sets of bushes reached by birds migrating south in autumn. Be careful of the bush crickets, as they sound very like grasshopper warblers. Beacon Lane and Easington lagoons are the only large areas of open water in the area, although Beacon Lane pool often dries up to a great extent in the summer. Many waders collect here at high tide, and flocks of dunlin feed actively over the exposed muddy areas.

In spring, flocks of ringed plover feed here as they stop over on their migration and many of them are of the northern tundra race.

In the winter, wigeon, teal, and mallard can be seen. Scarcer wildfowl also are seen there every winter such as pintail, scaup, and smew especially if the Baltic Sea freezes in a hard winter. There are many little pools and margins so a lot of patience is needed if you want to make the most of your time there. One such observer found a semi-palmated sandpiper, but it takes skill as well as patience to identify the rarest of waders when they are found. Not all of us are so fortunate, but you never know at Spurn.

There is a small colony of little terns that nest on the shingle there, but unfortunately they suffer a great deal of disturbance from holiday makers from the nearby caravan sites. Their nests are very vulnerable so please avoid this area during the breeding season.

Trees are few and far between in this windswept part of Holderness, so if you want to look for leaf warblers, then you should visit the local churches. The church graveyards at these villages have mature sycamore trees in them. These are a favourite haunt of pied fly catchers in autumn. If the winds have been in the north east at this time of year, then scarce Siberian warblers such as yellow-browed warbler and Pallas's warbler can sometimes be found. If you visit these graveyards please remember that you are on consecrated ground, even if you suspect that a dusky warbler has just darted around the back of a bush. And don't forget that the interior of these small churches have a charm of their own and deserve a visit as well.

If you are going to Sammy's Point, then you will pass Easington graveyard on the way to it. Sammy's is an area of open fields and scrub land along the edge of the estuary that runs back towards the local pub at Kilnsea. Brent geese feed on the mud flats here, and grey plover spread themselves thinly across the mud mixed in with dunlin, oystercatchers, redshank, curlew and all the other regular waders that frequent the Humber. Golden plover, ruff, and whimbrel can be seen in the fields there, particularly in spring, and after the crops have been cut. Ring ouzels can be flushed from the bushes on passage, and black redstarts too may be seen on the rocky areas. Be on the look out for dotterel amongst the golden plover in autumn; they are not in their best dress at this time of year, but it is always a treat to see them.

What ever the time of the year there are always lots of birds to see at this southernmost tip of Holderness, and the anticipation, and expectation of the unexpected, make this area one of the most important in the entire country. If you have not been there yet, then go.

Hornsea Mere   (Map Ref: 11).

This is an R.S.P.B. reserve that is part of the Strickland-Constable family estates. There is a full-time warden who monitors bird numbers here, and is also responsible for nearby Bempton Cliffs. It is a natural lake of some 300 acres, and has an island in the centre. There is a footpath along the western side which runs along an elevated bank that gives good views over the mere. There are large flocks of Canada, greylag, and barnacle geese at all times, although many of these are of suspicious origin, and probably come from Flamingoland zoo. It is not unusual to find hybrid birds among the flocks, and bar-headed geese are occurring more frequently. In winter there are large numbers of gadwall, mallard, wigeon, goldeneye etc. with smaller numbers of teal, and occasionally pintail. Great crested grebe numbers rise during the autumn, and red-necked or Slavonian grebe may also be encountered from time to time.

There is a good reedbed at the far end of the mere, and reed buntings, sedge warblers, reed warblers, and occasionally bearded reedling can be seen there. There is an area of woodland in this part as well, and green woodpecker and lesser spotted woodpecker are frequently sighted. Some of the trees have been blanched white with droppings from the large cormorant roost that is there each evening. Osprey has been reported from the reserve, and hen harriers and great grey shrike turn up from time to time, in the open countryside nearby. In recent years this has been a good place to see Mediterranean gull as a friendly bird has obliged visitors by feeding from the discarded remains of fish and chip portions, or the occasional sandwich thrown to it. It can be seen on the mere, but it seems to spend most of the day in the car park by the sea! Hornsea Bay is also a good place to watch from in the winter as both red-throated and black-throated divers pass along the coast.

Rafts of common scoter, together with the occasional velvet scoter, can usually be seen off shore. In autumn, manx shearwaters and sooty shearwaters ride the waves with the most effortless flight. Great skuas and arctic skuas move off their northern breeding grounds and fly south. These piratical birds will sometimes kill smaller sea birds given the chance.

So try to visit both the mere and the sea when you are at Hornsea. The warden takes parties around frequently upon request and in advance; you will get details of these escorted trips by writing to the R.S.P.B. or to the warden.

Bridlington Harbour and Bridlington Bay   (Map Ref: 12).

There is little doubt that from a birdwatching point of view the summer months here are best avoided as there are far too many holiday makers for comfortable birdwatching. The rest of the year is bracing and rewarding. Fishing boats arriving back from the sea always have a party of scavanging gulls behind them waiting for the remains of fish guts and heads to be cast over the side. In the early months of the year glaucous gulls are often amongst them and occasionally Iceland gulls. Later in the year great skuas often accompany the boats home. Purple sandpipers are especially confiding, and scamper over the rough rocks along the edge of the harbour and sea front walls. They are usually in the company of turnstones and redshanks and are best seen at high tide. After heavy seas it is often possible to see grebes in the harbour, and black guillemot, little auk and grey phalarope have also been seen there. Red-throated divers and great crested grebes move along the coast and can be seen from the harbour wall.

The bay sweeps southwards to Holderness and there are several places of interest on the way down that are always worth a visit.

Fraisthorpe   (Map Ref: 12).

Fraisthorpe beach has open fields behind it and flocks of golden plover congregate there in late autumn. Ringed plover and turnstones forage along the strand line for morsels, and sanderling follow the waves as the waters advance and recede. This can be a lonely stretch of beach, but some of the 'birds' there may turn out to be topless as this is also the local nude bathing beach. So be discrete as you scan the beach with your binoculars. The waters are cold all along this coast, so few people brave them on days other than the hottest.

Unfortunately the North Sea is not as friendly towards wildlife as it used to be, and there are more and more birds being found dead or dying on our beaches. This stretch often has the corpses of guillemots and other auks along the strand line. The guillemots are usually of the black northern race, and often there is no obvious sign of oiling. With the recent deaths of many seals in the North Sea, it is tempting to suggest that some form of pollution is affecting fish stocks and this is lowering their resistance to disease. It cannot be simply over fishing, as all species of fish seem to be affected. They are under sized, and often have lesions with missing scales. Most fish spawn in shallow waters such as along coastlines, and near estuaries to give protection to their fry in their early days. Here they can feed easily, but may also pick up pollutants that have been discharged sometimes many miles up the coast and washed south by the action of the sea. Whatever the truth is, it is leading to an increased mortality in both birds and mammals.

Barmston Cliffs   (Map Ref: 12).

Barmston cliffs are crumbling; they are made of boulder clay, and ammonites can often be found lying on the beach where there has been a land slip. Behind the shore there are open fields that extend inland to the Hull road, and a footpath runs north and south from the road end along the cliffs. Northwards it leads to a rough marsh with reed edges, and some standing water. In winter Brent geese can sometimes be seen here along with shelduck, wigeon, teal and mallard. Snipe, redshank and dunlin are often amongst the muddy pools. Some local birdwatchers have reported very rare passage waders here, so it is well worth a look. Off shore, large congregations of great crested grebes form in winter, and one or two red-necked or Slavonian grebes can usually be found. Scoter too can be seen here, usually further out to sea, and velvet scoter can be picked out with care, but it is not always easy as they seem to spend a lot of time behind the waves and only appear for a second at a time, before they disappear again.

This is a very good spot to see Lapland buntings and snow buntings. They can be present in large flocks, and a flock of 100 snow buntings can be a lovely sight as they rise into the winter air. Most winters there are usually one or two shore larks to be seen;

Black redstart.

these too can be hard to pick out as they are well camouflaged on shingle, but are well worth searching for.

The path to the south is worth trying as well, as the flocks of birds are very mobile and can cover large areas of land. Raptors such as merlin, peregrine, and hen harrier can turn up here throughout the winter, and short-eared owls quarter the saltings and open fields in the evenings.

Flamborough Head and South Landing   (Map Ref: 13).

East Yorkshire Borough Council has recently created a Heritage Trail at Flamborough and guided parties are taken by some of the local birdwatchers and ringers there in the summer months around South Landing and along the coastal footpath.

The headland is a chalk outcrop and juts out into the North Sea by about 5 miles. This seems to concentrate sea birds as they pass along the coast, which makes it one of the most important and best watched seawatching places in the country. Sea-watching is not for beginners to birdwatching as the birds are often far out to sea, and can only be seen with the aid of a good telescope. It takes years of experience to be able to identify birds in flight, and it is just not possible with a field guide in one hand and a pair of small binoculars in the other!

Kittiwakes are among the most numerous seen there and many thousands may pass per hour on a sea watch. In the early spring many of them can be seen with bills full of grass and mud to make crude nests on the rocky ledges that are all along this coastline. Guillemots are also very numerous, and together with smaller numbers of razorbills they compete for the remaining narrower clefts and ledges on the vertical slabs of rock that form the cliff face. The nests are not easy to see, so don't try to peer over as many have met a watery end there. House martins nest in small numbers around the headland in their traditional habitat. They must have nested on rocky walls before man built alternative cliff faces for them in towns.

Birds here could be passing along the coast for a number of reasons. Sea birds often travel in feeding parties either foraging, or returning to their nests with full crops; they could be on migration either to or away from their breeding grounds; or they may be wandering birds simply drifting around.

Red-throated and black-throated divers are seen there throughout the colder months, and in autumn hundreds of Manx shearwaters may be seen passing on a good day. If there has been a strong north-westerly wind, then sooty shearwaters turn up as well. Arctic skuas and great skuas [or Bonxies as birdwatchers call them] appear when there are parties of kittiwakes and Sandwich terns and common terns around. They harry them until they disgorge the contents of their crop, and the skua gets its ill-gotten meal of partly digested sand eels.

The best place to see small birds is South Landing. They find shelter and food there in the foliage as they arrive, come in off the sea, or as they move along the coast on migration. There is plenty of cover there, and goldcrests, willow warblers, whitethroats, blackcaps, as well as the unexpected migrants such as treecreepers may turn up. In autumn yellow-browed warblers, wryneck, barred warbler, icterine warbler, or red-backed shrike could be seen, and in springtime if you are really fortunate you may see a bluethroat there.

Among the shingle that lines the strand line, wading birds such as turnstone, redshank, knot, ringed plover, dunlin, and purple sandpipers may be seen in their season, searching through the dead wrack for insects and tiny crustacea. Many of the rocks among the shingle are chalk rocks and quite a few have holes bored through them. This has been done by a bivalve mollusc called a piddock that makes its home in the rock, and grinds its way in!

Thornwick Bay and North Landing   (Map Ref: 14).

If you are driving to Thornwick Bay then just before you get there you will see a muddy pool on your left that often has waders on it. There is a reed bed on the north side of the bay where reed and sedge warblers nest in the summer together with reed buntings, and in springtime grasshopper warblers often drop in before they continue their journey. In summer the cliffs have puffins nesting in old rabbit holes around the upper ledges, and the water is often full of razorbills and guillemots diving for food. They appear to fly under the water as they use their wings rather than their feet when they are swimming. In winter, divers may be seen close inshore drifting southwards feeding, and not infrequently red-necked grebes are spotted too.

The fields around the car park provide a feeding ground for corn buntings and yellowhammers, and in winter, snow buntings and Lapland buntings are seen in small numbers. Butterflies such as red admirals and painted ladies appear regularly all along the coast, and occasionally clouded yellows are seen here. The migratory moth silver Y can be very abundant in August, and can be seen flying during the daytime.

Danes Dyke   (Map Ref: 14).

This is an earth works that runs the length of Flamborough Head, and is overgrown with sycamore and other rapid colonisers. At the Sewerby end there is a ravine that is similar to the one at South Landing. They were both probably created by melt water from the retreating ice caps at the end of the last ice age which was finding its way to the sea. There is a substantial car park and a notice board with a map that shows the nature trails and walks there. A good view of the sweep of the bay down towards Bridlington can be seen from the top of the cliffs there, and this is also a good place for sea

Cliff "Climmers" after eggs in the 1920's at Bempton.

watching as there are eider, divers, and waders all along this stretch of coast. The woods are full of flowers in springtime, and all the regular woodland warblers that visit us are to be seen there together with treecreepers and woodpeckers.

Danes Dyke itself is thought to be part of an iron age fort.

Bempton Cliffs and Hoddy Cows Lane   (Map Ref: 15).

These towering cliffs are breath-takingly spectacular, and highly dangerous. Up until the early 1950's young men used to supplement their diet and income by descending the cliff on ropes to harvest guillemot, razorbill and kittiwake eggs. Most would be sold and eaten locally, but some would go to market, and would eventually find their way to the breakfast table in city homes. Egg collectors would assemble here each year, and would pay a handsome price for an unusually marked egg. This pursuit used to take place each year all along the sea cliffs of Yorkshire. Fortunately the law forbids this trade today.

Many souls have met their end here, and most of the cliffs are fenced off. However there are specially constructed viewing areas that the RSPB have built, which provide a safe place to see the thousands of guillemots and razorbills competing for the best nest ledges. Careful examination of the guillemots there will reveal that about 10% of them are of the 'bridled' form that have a white rim around the eye, and a white stripe that curves down and behind the eye. Puffins nest there in smaller numbers along the top of the cliff. Other nesting birds include fulmars and kittiwakes along the grassy ledges at the top, and shags which nest on the broader ledges at the bottom of the cliff.

Most people go to Bempton to see the gannetry. This is the only mainland nesting colony in the UK, and numbers have steadily increased since first breeding in 1937, to over 800 pairs in 1988.

Hoddy Cows Lane runs from the north of Buckton towards the sea. There are two small ponds at the start of the lane which occasionally have waders on their margin; but the most interesting aspect is the hedge and rambling scrub that borders the path. Migrant redstarts, black redstarts, pied flycatchers, and other songbirds come in off the sea exhausted and hungry for food in May and autumn. So check out this path if you are in the area.

Filey - The Bay, the Brigg and the Dams   (May Ref: 16).

Filey is a pleasant resort at all times of the year. It seems to cater for all tastes without losing its charm or character in the pursuit of the tourist. The town is elevated above the bay, and pleasant terraced gardens sweep down to the promenade which are ideal for warblers in the summer or on passage. There used to be a tea house at the tip of the Brigg that provided a welcome cuppa to the visitor who had made the walk to the end. Nowadays it is a hide for the local birdwatchers to sea-watch from. They provide the welcome now, and although this does not extend to a hot brew, they will be pleased to let you know what has been seen recently and invite you to join them if there is room in the hide. The hide is normally kept locked, but if you are on holiday there a key may be rented for the week from Filey Brigg Ornithological Group. Their address is in a later Chapter. Gannets, cormorants, shags, fulmars, auks etc. all pass across the end of the Brigg, and eiders are often seen close in shore. The bay provides an area of calmer water along a coast that can be savage in rough weather. Look out for red-throated divers, red-necked grebe, and long-tailed duck in the bay in winter. Kittiwakes, common terns, and Sandwich terns feed behind the breakers and are often robbed of their catch by passing skuas.

The Brigg is an interesting place for any naturalist, as there are excellent contrasts in habitat for marine organisms between the seaward side, and the bay side of the Brigg. Many 6th form biology classes go there to examine the zonation of racks between high and low water. But you do not need to be a student of marine ecology to turn over a few rocks, or to look at the animal life in the rock pools, and enjoy the diversity of life to be found there. There are brittle stars, chitons, blue-rayed limpets, sea lemons, and a host of other animals; so take a field guide to the sea shore with you as well as your binoculars!

Many of the birds there breed in the arctic and are quite unused to the presence of man. Purple sandpipers are especially confiding, and if you remain still they will often feed around your feet. Turnstone, dunlin, sanderling, knot, and other waders can also be seen well without optical aids.

At the top of the Brigg is Filey Country Park. This is where many waders roost overnight, and up to 100 redshank may be seen feeding at dusk. There is an area that has been planted out with *rosa ruggosa* and other small shrubs. They always have flocks of linnet and greenfinch in attendance, and in spring and autumn often have much rarer birds to be found! In the past few years Radde's warbler, greenish warbler, Pallas's warbler, collared flycatcher, and red-throated pipit have been seen. In the colder months snow buntings feed on the Brigg, Lapland buntings can often be heard calling as they fly over, and shore larks can sometimes be found in the ploughed fields.

Near the cafe there is a small ravine called Arndale where there is easy access to the beach. This is also well provided with cover and icterine warbler, and wryneck turn up most years. There is a small team of ringers there who are very active in the autumn and their recoveries provide a valuable insight into coastal migration.

Don't forget to check out the trees that line the ravine that leads down to the Coble Landing. It is very good for birds, and is not watched as regularly as the other spots in Filey.

The Dams   (Map Ref: 16).

This is a newly created reserve that has been made with the enthusiasm of the local birdwatchers and local authorities. It is now one of Yorkshire Wildlife Trust's reserves. There is a hide which looks out onto a scrape, and there are always teal, mallard, snipe, and moorhen around. Garganey and black redstart are seen annually, and sparrowhawk and short-eared owls may be seen at most times of the year. Pellets disgorged by the owls have revealed that their diet is mainly field voles. Olive-backed pipit, rustic bunting, purple heron, and night heron have also called in during the last few years. But don't go to Filey in the expectation of seeing something unusual on every visit, just be content to enjoy your birdwatching in one of the most pleasant towns on the coast.

Cornelian Bay   (Map Ref: 17).

This bay lies just to the north of the popular tourist spot Cayton Bay, but as access to Cornelian Bay is very steep, and as there are no silver sands there, few trippers bother to visit it. This is fortunate, because it is a very attractive bay to both sea and land birds. Eider feed from the mussel beds there, and mergansers, shags, and divers can often be seen diving for fish. In the winter it is a popular place for goldeneye, and wading birds are always plentiful at all times of the year. Knot, purple sandpipers, redshank and dunlin can be seen at the sewage outlet in their season, and terns feed along with the kittiwakes in summer.

The bay is wooded down to the edge of the beach, and blackcaps, garden warblers, chiffchaff and other common warblers may be seen throughout the summer. Cuckoo frequent the trees looking for the unguarded dunnock nest, and both green and great spotted woodpeckers are there.

Great skua chasing a young kittiwake.

Scarborough Harbour and the North Headland   (Map Ref: 18).

Tell her to plough me an acre of land,
Parsley, sage, rosemary and thyme,
Between the salt water and the sea strand.
And then she'll be a true love of mine.
[Scarborough Fair]

The harbour at Scarborough is very active, and there are always plenty of vessels moving in and out with the tide. The trawlers off-load their haul at the fish wharf and herring gulls and great black-backed gulls are always waiting for scraps to be tossed aside. During the winter they are joined by glaucous gulls and occasionally Iceland gulls. These white winged-gulls are very easy to pick out among the other darker birds as they accompany the boats home, or sit on top of the houses waiting for the next to come into port. The harbour provides a sanctuary for storm driven birds to recouperate, and red-necked and black-necked grebe, guillemots and sometimes little auks or black guillemot can be seen there. The beach is usually crowded, but in the winter, sanderlings and dunlin freely roam the water's edge, and purple sandpipers and turnstones frequent the Spa end of the shore where it is more rocky.

The castle at Scarborough is well planted with trees, and willow warblers, chiffchaff, whitethroats and other warblers may be seen throughout the summer. In the autumn, yellow-browed warbler, barred warbler, red-backed shrike, red-breasted flycatcher, pied flycatchers and redstarts have been seen regularly. The cliffs there are massive and crumbling and thousands of kittiwakes nest there each year. Fulmars have extended their breeding range southwards this century, and many nest here, and all along the east coast where there are cliffs. There is a very pretty moth called a magpie moth, that can often be seen flying in the daytime in the bushes around the headland.

Scalby Mills and Jackson's Bay   (Map Ref: 19).

Tell her to find me a sewage outlet,
Partridge, quail, rosefinch and twite.
With Sabine's gull, Ross's and crested auklet,
And then she'll be a true love of mine!
[*Anon*]

There has been a sewage outlet here for many years where largely untreated sewage has been discharged into the sea in the hope that the sea would somehow dispose of it. Most of this simply washed back onto the beach at high tide, and presented an offensive and hazardous mess to the bathing public. At the moment a new pumping plant is being constructed at Scalby Mills to be commissioned in 1991. The idea is simply to screen off the solid materials and render the rest into a slurry. Then the sewage slurry is to be pumped about 1500 metres out into the sea so that there is less chance of it being washed back. The hope is that the sea will act as an unlimited bio-degrading system and will render the waste harmless without any long term damage to the marine life there! There are sewage outfalls all along the North Sea, and to date the Government has not kept pace with our European neighbours in reducing the amount of raw sewage that is dumped. The natural drift of the tides along the east coast is bound to return much of what is discharged, and with the particle sizes being much smaller in the future the risk of illness to bathers may increase as they will not be able to see the hazzards in the water.

The discharges in the past have at least attracted large flocks of kittiwakes, black-headed gulls, and herring gulls that have fed on the outflow at high tide. From time to time rare gulls such as Sabine's gull and Ross's gull have been seen here and Mediterranean gull and little gulls are frequently seen.

Jackson's bay is the small bay to the north of Scalby Mills, and goldeneye, red-breasted merganser, and eider feed there. Grey phalarope has been recorded in several winters, and the rocky margins are a good place to see redshank, dunlin, turnstone, curlew, and in the cold part of the year, purple sandpipers.

The beck Sea Cut flows into the sea here, and kingfishers have sometimes been seen there, as has the black-bellied form of dipper which is a continental bird. There is an area of scrub behind the headland which has linnets, yellowhammers, and meadow pipits throughout the year. This spot also has slow worms among the course thick grasses, and they can sometimes be seen crossing the paths or be found asleep under stones or logs.

North Yorkshire Coast   (Map Ref: 20).

There are far too many tiny inlets and bays here to try to describe them all, so I shall leave it up to the reader to explore some of them for his, or herself, and discover some of the delightful places there. As one travels further up the coast there are more mussel beds, as there is less effluence discharged. So there are lots more eiders and scoters to be seen. The river Esk flows into the harbour at Whitby, and the fishing boats attract flocks of gulls. The rocks at Robin Hood's Bay are a good place to look for waders such as turnstones and purple sandpipers, and the bushes on the cliffs attract passage migrants. Kettleness is another place that has great potential for birdwatchers, as it is a good place for seawatching and many migrants drop in there in spring and autumn. Boggle Hole has a small stream running down to the beach, and has plenty of cover for songbirds to shelter in, on the gulley sides. The harbour village of Staines attracts many photographers, and appears on calendars each year. If you are in the area, call in and sample the local hospitality, and take a stroll down the sea front: you will find that there are always plenty of birds to see there too.

If you are lucky you may find jet along the beaches near Whitby. This is a variety of lignite, and is carved into ornaments and jewellery by local craftsmen. It is easy to mistake pieces of coal that have been smoothed by the waves for jet, as lots of coal is washed down the coast from Northumberland where there is still a disgraceful amount of coastal dumping.

So enjoy this unspoiled strip of Yorkshire's coastline, the winds are fresh, the crab sandwiches are tasty, the ale is strong, and the birdwatching is excellent.

Scaling Dam   (Map Ref: 21).

This is a reservoir on the main Whitby-Guisborough road that was built in the 1920's to provide water to Teesside. It is used for several leisure activities such as sailing as well as for birdwatching. There is a large gull roost each evening, and glaucous and Iceland gulls are seen each winter. Regular watchers have also seen little gulls and Mediterranean gulls there. The reservoir also attracts a lot of wildfowl, and as it is so close to the sea, keep an eye out for the occasional scaup or pintail or common scoter. Waders frequent the margin, and little stint and curlew sandpiper have turned up. There is a hide that overlooks the north end of the reservoir and the moors. In winter hen harriers are recorded regularly from this hide. The list is far too long to relate all the interesting birds seen there, but Wilson's phalarope and Terek sandpiper are among them.

The River Tees and Teesmouth   (Map Ref: 22)

The Tees has its source in upper Teesdale which is one of the richest botanical sites in the country; with plants such as Alpine bartsia, Mountain avens, Teesdale violet, and other very rare Alpine plants. Many of these plants are found exclusively in upper Teesdale. Unfortunately many sites were lost when Cow Green reservoir was constructed to provide water for industry in Teesmouth. Ironically the anticipated demand for water was not met, as demand for heavy industrial products fell.

The river cascades out of the reservoir and over a very hard ancient rock intrusion, called the Great Whin Sill, at Cauldron

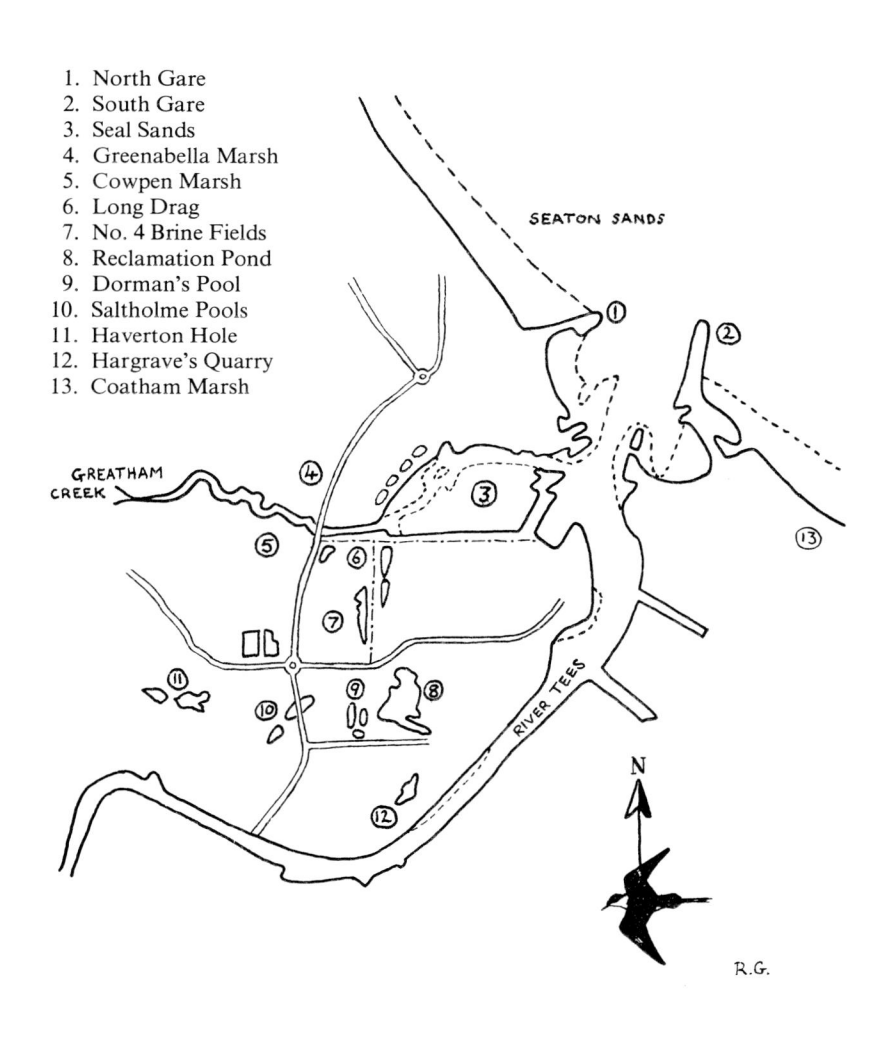

1. North Gare
2. South Gare
3. Seal Sands
4. Greenabella Marsh
5. Cowpen Marsh
6. Long Drag
7. No. 4 Brine Fields
8. Reclamation Pond
9. Dorman's Pool
10. Saltholme Pools
11. Haverton Hole
12. Hargrave's Quarry
13. Coatham Marsh

Teesmouth & Seal Sands

Snout. It then flows rapidly down to High Force and on to the lowlands. As with most rivers, the waters are clean and pure in the upper reaches, and many a thirsty traveller has refreshed himself from the river. Lower down the waters contain insidious ions. Nitrates and phosphates from surrounding farmland enrich the nutrient content of the river, and encourage algae growths. Rain water deposits a weakly acidic solution into the river, and this has the ability to free lead salts that have accumulated in the bed of the river from ancient washings at old lead mines. By the time the river reaches Teesmouth it would be a foolish person who drank from the water there, as heavy industry adds its load to the already overburdened river.

There are now no places on Teesmouth where one may stand free from the presence of industry. The country needs industry, and without it we would have no services, but the price of this is high in terms of the waste the rivers have to carry, and this must improve if we are to restore the quality of our environment. ICI and other industries have reduced the biological and chemical oxygen demand placed on the river over the past 15 years. But there is still a long way to go, and there are many new, and potentially more toxic chemicals being found in marine organisms, so the problems are far from being solved. This is one area where industry should take a positive lead.

ICI have several very interesting sites on their land, and it is to their credit that they have made an effort to maintain them and encourage the public to visit them and see industry and conservation together, if not yet in harmony.

South Gare   (Map Ref: 22).

> *A've walked at neet through Sheffield lanes,*
> *'twere t'same as bein' in Hell.*
> *Furnaces thrust up tongues of fire*
> *That roared like the winds off t'fell*
> *An' a've sammed up coal in Barnsley pits*
> *Wi' muck up to my knee.*
> *From Hull an' Halifax an' Hell,*
>   *good Lord deliver me.*
> [*Dalesman's Litany*]

This is an industrial landscape, and is one of the best places for bird watching on South Teesside. It can be reached by taking the road to the steel works from Redcar. There is a small harbour there and a lighthouse overlooking the bay and the mouth of the river. In winter there are wigeon and goldeneye to be seen and seals are regularly reported. Cormorants dive for eels there, and red-throated divers often join them. Skuas and shearwaters can be seen in autumn, and little gulls pass in small numbers throughout the late summer.

There are rough grassy areas behind the dunes that are worth exploring in spring and autumn, as bluethroat and ring ousels are found each spring. These dunes extend all along the coastal strip beyond Redcar, through Marske and on to the bay before the headland at Saltburn. Between the steel works and the dunes there are teal, wigeon and other wildfowl to be found in the pools near the golf course. The area does not look promising at first glance, but it is well worth the effort of thoroughly working it.

From the lighthouse one may look out to sea, or view the mouth of the Tees as it widens out across to Seal Sands. The gulls there often roost on the sides and the masts of the boats in the harbour, so always scan them to check for Mediterranean or little gull in summer, and glaucous or Iceland gull in winter.

Coatham Marsh   (Map Ref: 22).

This is a newly created reserve at Redcar that is managed by Cleveland Nature Trust for Conservation. The area is well flooded, and wading birds such as snipe and redshank as well as teal, mallard, wigeon, and tufted duck can be seen. There are public hides that overlook the water, and records of the birds you have seen there will be welcomed. They have had some scarce birds in the past few years, with black-winged stilt, little egret, and blue-winged teal. Less rare birds can be just as nice to watch, and appear much more reliably, such as reed buntings, and little grebes which are always present.

If you are in the area, then Locke Park is worth a visit particularly in autumn when yellow-browed warblers are regularly seen.

Saltholme Pools, Dorman's Pool and Reclamation pool
(Map Ref: 22).

These pools are on ICI land, and they have agreed to leave this land undeveloped and left as a nature reserve. It forms part of the North Tees marshes that includes Long Drag, and Cowpen Marsh. The land is rough and marshy and attracts very large numbers of waders, gulls, and wildfowl.

Lapwing, golden plover, and black-headed gulls can be abundant. Ruff, greenshank, dunlin, and redshank can also be present in double figures. The birds may be seen closely either from the roadway that overlooks Saltholme pools, or from the hide at Dorman's. The hide is not always open, as it belongs to Teesmouth Bird Club, but if it is open then they will make you welcome if there is room. Reclamation pool can be seen well from the top of the track that leads to Dorman's pool, and attracts lots of shelduck and curlew.

In autumn, little stint and curlew sandpipers are regular visitors. At first sight this is another place that does not look all that promising, but there are regular highlights in every year here. Wilson's phalarope, Boneparte's gull, American lesser golden plover, have all been seen in the past 10 years, as well as one or two colourful birds of questionable origin such as Chilean flamingo and ruddy shelduck. A long-toed stint constituted the first ever record for Britain here. There is a flower here that is very common called wall rocket. It is a member of the cabbage family and has small yellow petals. It is unusual in that it is one of our few flowers that has a very nasty smell when picked.

Long Drag to Seal Sands   (Map Ref: 22).

Long Drag is a shale track that runs the length of the ICI brine fields. There are more pools and lagoons here, but as the track is elevated the birds are much easier to see provided you do not disturb them as you walk down it. Ringed plovers breed here, as do many pairs of common terns. They can be seen carrying sand eels in their bills in spring as they perform their courtship displays; sand eels are important to terns as they constitute a major part of their diet. In autumn they are joined by Sandwich terns as they migrate south. Arctic skuas always accompany them and they are always chasing the terns for a free meal. Every year hen harrier, marsh harrier, peregrine, merlin, and hobby are seen here, and osprey and black kite have been seen occasionally too. Both of these rarer raptors have been expanding their range and are being seen more frequently. Ospreys have made a successful return to these isles, and black kites are spreading west in Europe, so with luck we will be seeing more of them in the future.

Further down Long Drag there are some deeper lagoons that have wigeon, teal, pochard, shoveller, pintail, shelduck, etc., and most years garganey is reported. Grey herons fish here, and bar-tailed godwits, grey plover, and whimbrel can be seen each passage. After you have reached the end of Long Drag you will be ready to sit down, and fortunately there is a hide there where you will be able to scan the vast expanse of Seal Sands. Here you can see thousands of waders at low tide, and as the tide rises, the birds become more and more concentrated, and are eventually driven to flight, to roost along Long Drag or along the North Tees Marshes. In winter goldeneye and mergansers can be seen along with cormorants and the odd red-throated diver. If it has been a long walk down Long Drag, then it always seems further on the way back, but there is always the chance that you will see something that you missed on the way down.

Cowpen Marsh and Greatham Creek   (Map Ref: 22).

Greatham Creek winds its way across Cowpen Marsh and drains into Seal Sands. It is a tidal creek, and as the water fills the estuary many waders move up Greatham Creek before they eventually fly off to roost. There are two hides that over look the creek and they give very good views of ruff, greenshank, and other waders as they feed. Golden plover, snipe and jack snipe frequent the fields of Cowpen Marsh in winter, and hen harriers, merlins, kestrels etc., can be seen hunting. Cowpen Marsh used to be an RSPB reserve, but is now managed by Cleveland Nature Trust for Conservation.

Rough-legged buzzard at Roseberry Topping.

North Yorks Moors (Map Ref: 23).

This ay neet, this ay neet,
Ivry neet and ahl.
Fire and fleet and candle leet,
And Christ receive thy sahl.
[*Lyke Wake Dirge*]

There are several places that are worth visiting here if only to view the beauty of the area. In many respects it resembles parts of the Yorkshire Dales, but it retains its own charm and character without the volume of traffic that chokes the Dales roads in summer. Many hardened walkers tackle the Lyke Wake Walk each year, which crosses the moore from Osmotherly in the west to Ravenscar on the coast. But for the birdwatcher and naturalist there are different attractions. In springtime wild daffodils bloom on the wooded hillsides around Farndale, and dotterel regularly break their migration northwards at Rosedale. Ring ouzel occur throughout the summer months and although they are more secretive than their lowland relative the blackbird, they always seem quite numerous. The moors have a fair population of red grouse, and meadow pipits are abundant here. Red grouse are found naturally only in these isles, although they have a continental cousin called willow grouse. They succeed best on managed moors where there is a good crop of heather and bilberry each year. Merlins are recorded regularly each summer, and peregrines are being seen more often. There are several pairs that nest in the West Riding, and hopefully this range expansion will soon occur here. Peregrines used to nest on coastal cliffs at Flamborough.

In winter there is a hen harrier roost, and Bransdale and Westerdale are places that are regularly visited by birdwatchers in the hope of seeing rough-legged buzzard, but in recent years there have been fewer records. This is possibly due to milder winters which have led to fewer birds moving south.

The Yorkshire Wolds

It was pleasant and delightful one midsummer's morn,
When the fields and the meadows were covered with corn.
There were blackbirds and thrushes that sang on every
  green sway,
And the larks they sang melodious at the dawning of
  the day.
[Pleasant and delightful - traditional]

These are an intersecting network of dry chalk valleys that run northwards from the Humber, and then east towards Flamborough Head. They are steep sided and flat bottomed and were formed during a period of intense glaciation. This has resulted in some very attractive south facing valleys that hold numerous chalk downland flowers such as carline thistle, and clustered bellflower. There are also numerous colonies of common blue, and a few marbled white butterflies may sometimes be seen on knapweed there. The valleys often have scattered hawthorn scrub which act as song posts for whinchat, redstart, tree pipit, whitethroat and lesser whitethroat. Yellowhammers and corn buntings are seen along the telephone wires and hedgerows. In winter there are a few spots that regularly have a roost of long-eared owls. One valley often has a roost of a dozen or so birds, but it is difficult to say whether these are British birds or Continental immigrants, as many long-eared owls come into this country from Scandinavia in late autumn.

There are many public rights of way in this area, and some run through some of the most picturesque of Yorkshire countryside, such as at Millington pastures which is itself an SSSI. A countryside ranger employed by Humberside County Council is responsible for the development of Millington Woods, and a most sympathetic approach has been adopted towards the need to establish a balanced natural environment out of a badly managed woodland. Local schools have erected many nest boxes in the woods, and most are used by blue tits and great tits. Some of these are destined to provide a meal for the pair of sparrowhawk and their young that also nest there. A public viewing hide and a bird feeding station are to be created in the near future.

Forge Valley   (Map Ref: 24).

There are several areas in the east of Yorkshire that are wooded and are relatively undisturbed, so that the undercover is not removed, and fallen timber is left to decay naturally with the help of saprophytic fungi and other decomposers. This has enabled the local bird populations to develop with little detrimental interference from man. In fact in the Forge Valley area outside Scarborough local bird lovers have provided food on a regular basis for many years now, and the birds have become to some extent dependant upon the provision of food for them especially when times are hard. There are feeding areas in lay-bys along the road and the birds there are remarkably confiding. Chaffinches, nuthatches, blue and great tits will feed very close to parked cars, and if you put a tray of seed on the bonnet of your car they will feed from it. It is not at all unusual for a great spotted woodpecker, jay, coal tit or treecreeper to be seen in the trees there.

Dalby Forest   (Map Ref: 25).

There are two YNT reserves that can be visited in this locality that are easily viewed from the Dalby Forest Drive.

Ellerburn Bank is near Thornton Dale, and although its main interest is of a botanical and entomological nature, there are plenty of adders, and lots of birds to see. Kestrels and sparrowhawks breed around there, and grey herons call in at the nearby trout hatchery. From time to time ospreys stop over in spring, and help themselves to the odd free meal. There are crossbills in the forest, but they are not easy to locate and are best seen in the winter when they move around in small flocks before they start breeding in February.

Bridestones is woodland and upland pasture and has a different character from the lower part of the forest. There are deciduous trees here, and birds typical of this type of woodland are plentiful. The Dalby forest is one of the last strongholds of nightjar in Yorkshire. For complete details of walks around the forest, and all other Forestry Commission woodlands, write to 1a Grosvenor Terrace, York.

Tophill Low   (Map Ref: 26).

The site is one of Yorkshire Water Authority's abstraction and treatment works. It is situated on the river Hull, and lies between Beverley and Driffield. Aside from the treatment plant there are two large holding tanks called the 'D' and the 'O' reservoirs, where water is stored before treatment. There are two areas of marsh, and some shallow pools that are the remains of previous excavation work. The 'D' reservoir is the larger of the two, and a substantial hide built on stilts overlooks it. It attracts good numbers of wildfowl in winter with mallard, pochard, tufted duck being well represented, as well as smaller numbers of teal, wigeon, gadwall, goldeneye, shoveller, shelduck and goosander. There are usually a few winter records of the scarcer grebes such as Slavonian or red-necked, and occasionally red-throated divers are seen. There are increasing records of ruddy duck which are spreading throughout Yorkshire, and a regular visitor has been a ring-necked duck that turned up each winter during the 80's.

Occasionally these holding tanks are drained to be cleaned out, and they then pull in very large numbers of passage waders such as ruff, green sandpipers, dunlin, redshank, greenshank, and spotted redshank.

The marshes are also good for waders at all times of the year with regular visits from all the common passage birds. Less common birds are also regularly seen here such as water rail which is a breeding bird, and spotted crake. Each of the marshes has its own hide.

Recently a large amount of clay has been removed from Watton Borrows Pit, and this has created a flooded area that has provided a nesting site for great crested grebe, and ringed plovers. The area is not easy to view, but future plans for the reserve include an elevated viewing platform.

Records are kept on a daily basis, so please don't forget to record all that you see, in the log book in the reception hut. These will help in the creation of the annual report which may be purchased whilst you are there.

Access is restricted to permit holders who are members of the recently formed Tophill Low Wildlife Group. Details of membership can be obtained from Paul Bishop, 29 Beech View, Hutton Cranswick, Driffield.

Alternatively, a day permit may be applied for in advance.

Castle Howard Lakes (Map Ref: 27).

She stepped away from me and she moved through the fair,
And fondly I watched her move here and move there.
And then she went homewards with one star awake,
As the swan in the evening moves over the lake.
[She moved through the fair]

There are very few lakes in central Yorkshire, and although the three here are ornamental lakes, the largest of them attracts good numbers of wildfowl throughout the year. It is surrounded by trees and flocks of mixed tits move and feed freely around the lake. There are flocks of Canada and greylag geese that are often joined in the winter months by white fronted, pinkfoot, and bean gease. Wigeon and teal and goosander may also be seen in the winter, and occasionally divers such as great northern call in here. There is a reed-bed at the House end of the lake, where herons often fish, that leads to a smaller lake that holds reed and sedge warblers in summer. Access to the lake is via a footpath from the road. There is a nice lily covered lake inside the grounds that is a favourite spot for hirundines throughout the summer months. Spotted flycatcher, great spotted and green woodpeckers can be seen in the grounds, and in the last century, ravens nested regularly on the mausoleum.

Strensall Common   (Map Ref: 28).

'Twas on a summer's morning as I rode o'er the moss,
I had no thoughts of enlisting 'till some soldiers did
me cross.
They kindly did invite me to a flowing bowl in town,
And they advanced me some money, a shilling of the crown.
[*The white cockade - Traditional*]

This reserve lies in the Vale of York, and is one of the largest areas of heathland left in this part of the county. In the summer there are whinchats, tree pipits, curlew and woodcock to be seen, as well as many adders. They bask in the warmth of the sun and feed on the lizard population and any small mammals that they can find. The land was purchased from the Ministry of Defence some years ago, and may be entered from the Flaxton road. There are open areas with ling and bracken, stands of silver birch, and wet areas where in autumn, marsh gentian blooms, and makes a splendid picture. Long-eared owl and nightjar have both bred here in recent years.

Wheldrake Ings   (Map Ref: 29).

There are two public viewing hides overlooking the reserve which was purchased by Yorkshire Wildlife Trust in 1971 as an important flood meadow. The lower Derwent used to run around the north and east of the reserve towards Pocklington Canal, but in the past it was changed to its present route. The reserve floods from early winter through into late spring, although some area of standing water is present throughout the year. Bewick swans and whooper swans occur every winter and stay until April. Shoveller, wigeon, pintail, goosander, and resident flocks of greylag and Canada geese may also be seen here. Each year, garganey, smew, red-breasted merganser and bean goose are also recorded, as too are merlin, hen harrier, short-eared owl, and barn owl.

Goldeneye and Wigeon at Wheldrake Ings.

The fields here are old hay meadows that have not been reseeded for centuries and contain a rich variety of native grasses and sedges. They are classed as SSSI's and are not cut until the middle of July, so it gives ground nesting birds a chance to raise their young without disturbance, and the plants time to shed their seed. Grey partridges occur in smaller numbers than their continental cousin, red-legged partridge. Quail and corncrake, which have only a tenuous toe hold in this country, have also been recorded there.

Wading birds turn up during passage, and whimbrel, curlew, and green sandpipers can be seen there. On the wet grassy fields, flocks of lapwing and golden plover feed along with snipe and redshank.

The river bank has been replanted with willow in several stretches, and sedge warblers, reed buntings and kingfishers occur. So too do green woodpeckers, great spotted and lesser spotted woodpeckers, and jays which breed in nearby woodland. Great grey shrike has also been seen there in several recent winters.

Lower Derwent to North Duffield Carrs   (Map Ref: 30).

This area stretches from Wheldrake Ings in the north to Bubwith Ings and North Duffield Carrs in the south. The meadows bloom, with a multitude of wild flowers of many different species in summer, so many stretches are classed as SSSI's. All along the margin of the Derwent there are snipe, reed buntings, meadow pipits, curlew, and redshank, with smaller numbers of shelduck, and oystercatcher. There is a colony of black-headed gulls at Ellerton, where mallard and greylag geese breed. The best place to go to however is the Geoff Smith hide at North Duffield Carrs. It is situated along the Bubwith to Selby road, with a good car park. The hide was erected by the Nature Conservancy Council with the help of York Birdwatchers Club. The hide overlooks a scrape which has been dug out, and attracts little ringed plovers, redshank and many other wading birds. Small passerines such as goldfinch and linnet also call in to drink there, and to feed on seeds around the water's edge.

It is a good place to look out for birds that are migrating up the Derwent, as whimbrel, dunlin, greenshank, and terns are regularly seen there and often stop off at the scrape before continuing their journey. Flocks of golden plover are very mobile and move up and down the entire length of the Derwent from August to Spring.

In winter this is an excellent place to see wildfowl, as large numbers of wigeon and teal feed and roost along the river. It is also a good place to see both whooper and Bewick's swans which over winter from Bubwith to Wheldrake. Birds of prey regularly turn up and hen harrier, merlin, and occasionally peregrine are seen. This part of the country is one of the few strongholds of barn owl, which may be seen at any time of the day during the winter, and hunt for voles etc. across the fields in the early summer evenings when they have young to feed.

Allerthorpe Common   (Map Ref: 31)

This area lies to the north west of Allerthorpe village near Pocklington. It used to consist of over 100 acres of open heathland covered with heather and isolated patches of silver birch. Only 15 acres remain and are managed by Yorkshire Wildlife Trust. The rest have been planted with Scots, Corsican, and Lodgepole Pine with

a) Mallard (*Anas platyrhynchos*) posing on the Ouse bank near York.
b) Spotted flycatcher (*Muscicapa striata*) feeding young at Givendale.
c) Barn owl (*Tyto alba*) chick receiving its B.T.O. ring which will identify it if it is found again.

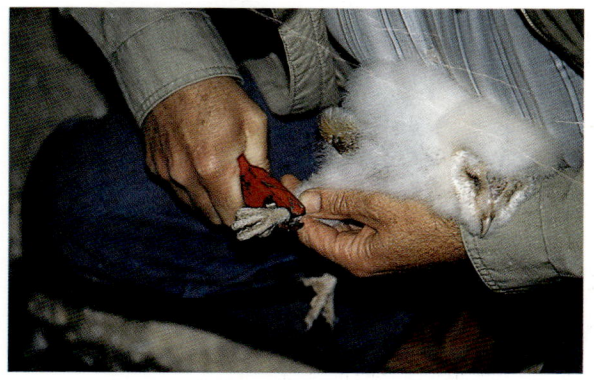

a) Woodcock (*Scolopax rusticola*) well camouflaged amongst dead leaves and bracken.
b) Sparrowhawk (*Accipiter nisus*) feeding three youngsters.
c) Coal tit (*Parus ater*). They often come to bird tables in winter.

some Western Hemlock. This has completely changed the character of the area and greatly reduced the number and variety of birds to be seen there. The main loss has been nightjar which has not been seen since the early 80's, but also, curlew, redstart, and winchat have been lost as breeding species. There have been some gains, however, as crossbills and long-eared owls have bred there in recent years. There are also good numbers of breeding coal tit, goldcrest, tree pipit, and woodcock.

There is an excellent pool within the reserve that holds good numbers of both smooth and palmate newts; some of their tadpoles feed the great diving beetles. In the summer there are lots of damselflies and dragonflies hawking for smaller insects over the water. Marsh cinquefoil is abundant around the edge of the pool, and grass wave, a rare Yorkshire moth, may be seen flying around the heather in summer. Other moths of interest are emperor, drinker, and clouded buff.

The site also contains many adders, so do not go there with your dog, as it may get bitten. There are also glow worms to be seen in the late summer evenings, but take some insect repellent with you, as the mosquitoes are always hungry!

Pocklington Canal and the surrounding areas   (Map Ref: 32).

Pocklington canal is about 12 miles in length, and flows from Canal Head on the west of the town, to the river Derwent at East Cottingwith. It is an old transport canal that fell into disuse in the middle of the last century when it was taken over by the York and North Midlands Railway Company. It is still navigable up to the village of Melbourne, but above there the locks are in a poor state of repair although efforts have been made by Pocklington Canal Amenity Group to restore the top lock recently.

Since its closure as a commercial waterway, there has been little to discourage the colonisation of the margins with reeds and reed mace. Consequently there are always reed buntings flitting along the bank, and in the summer there are equal numbers of reed and sedge warbler. The entire canal has now been notified as a SSSI as it is rich in aquatic plants. Red-eyed damselfly can be seen there which is very rare in Yorkshire. In winter large mixed flocks of redpoll and siskin can be seen foraging amongst the alder trees that line several stretches of the canal.

The meadows that surround the canal from Melbourne and Thornton to East Cottingwith have not been re-sown for many centuries and as well as having a rich and diverse flora, hold many waders in the spring. Snipe can be seen and heard drumming all along these meadows, and redshank and curlew call constantly from them as they establish their territories. Many pass through on their way to higher ground, but a significant number stay on to nest.

During the winter months thousands of wildfowl feed along the River Derwent, and many teal, wigeon, mallard, and shelduck find their way along the canal and into these fields. Barn owl may also be seen along the canal hunting the fields at any time of the year.

There is a slurry pit that is always worth a look at in Melbourne owned by East Yorkshire Farm Produce that attracts, in particular, green sandpipers that often over winter in this region. The spot is a bit smelly, but a white-rumped sandpiper did not seem to mind in 1983!

Seavy Carr (Map Ref: 32).

This is an area of wetland of about 80 acres, owned by the NCC just outside the village of Thornton on the north side of Pocklington canal. Eventually this is intended to be designated a national nature reserve, and a scrape and a public viewing hide is to be created to try to tempt some of the large numbers of waders that frequent the area to drop in and be seen at close quarters. At the moment it has a good selection of breeding wetland warblers including grasshopper warblers. Some of the many meadow pipits in the area and some of the reed warblers along Pocklington canal become host parents for the many cuckoos that frequent the area in spring and early summer. In the winter large roaming flocks of siskin often feed in the alders there, and smaller flocks of corn buntings, yellowhammers and bramblings frequent the hawthorns. Up to 100 snipe have been recorded in the winter together with jack snipe which is not at all uncommon in this area. Short-eared owl and honey buzzard have also been reported from this reserve in recent years.

a) Herring gull (*Larus argentotus*) eggs hatching out on an East Coast cliff.
b) Arctic tern (*Sterna paradisaea*) ringed on the Farne Islands as a youngster.
c) Greenfinch (*Carduelis chloris*) a quarrelsome feeder at peanut bags in winter gardens.

a) A family of four young swallows (*Hirund rustica*) waiting to be fed.
b) Evening sunset with a group of mute swans.
c) Puffins (*Fratercula arctica*) at their nest burrows on the coast.

a)

b)

c)

Jack snipe.

Skipwith Common   (Map Ref: 33).

This is an extensive area of silver birch with some open pools, and cleared heath. The heath has a good carpet of heather on it but there is always the threat of advancing silver birch which would engulf the heath were it not to be checked and cut back regularly. Silver birch spreads as easily from suckers from the root stock as it does by seed.

Most birdwatchers go to the common in the evenings during late May and early June, as nightjar can be seen displaying and hawking for moths and other insects over the heath. There is plenty for them to eat as there are clouds of irritating midges and biting mosquitoes there, so do not forget to take some insect repellent with you. Long-eared owls can be heard calling in spring, and the squeaky calls of their chicks waiting to be fed can always be heard in June and July. The birch trees provide food for large parties of redpoll, and siskin have been seen there in winter. Tree pipits sing from the birches and cuckoos are plentiful in summer, no doubt looking for the nests of inattentive meadow pipits. Grasshopper warblers breed in smaller numbers but are never easy to see.

Heather growth seems to be improved by regular burning, and although the immediate consequences to nature seem profound, a severe fire that swept the heath some years ago has brought renewed life to it through regeneration. Irregular burning seems to be one of the best ways of ensuring the continuation of our native heathlands, which, in the past must have been done by lightning strikes.

Bishop Wood

This wood is situated near Selby, and has several nature trails that may be explored. The paths are broad, and there is a good underbrush that has several species of orchid in spring and summer, and lots of tangled honeysuckle. It is when you see honeysuckle entwined around the branches of other trees that the old country name 'woodbine' becomes meaningful. Coal tits, wrens, chaffinches, and treecreepers are common, and sparrowhawks can often be seen hunting through the tops of the trees. Crossbills are reported occasionally, and probably breed in small numbers.

In winter flocks of redwings and fieldfare scavenge the remains of autumn's fruit crops, and any haws that are left are quickly stripped. Woodmice are common there and they clean up any hazel nuts that fall. Squirrels are not liked by foresters as they can scar trees with their claws, and break off growing shoots as they gnaw the young branches in search of sap. In recent years a much more serious threat to plantations has been roaming flocks of roe deer. These lovely animals can do a lot of damage to young trees as they nibble away the growing branches. But this is surely a small price to pay for their presence in our countryside.

a) A young owl being fed on a green caterpillar.
b) Moorhen (*Gallinula chloropus*) raising its tail as a warning to the photographer!
c) This chaffinch (*Fringilla coelebs*) is short of water, and having to eat snow.

a) Feed me! young song thrushes (*Turdus philomelos*).
b) Female kestrel (*Falco tinnunculus*) bringing food to hungry mouths.
c) Shags (*Phalacrocorax aristotelis*) breed all along rocky sea cliffs.

OTHER PLACES OF INTEREST

It has not been possible to cover every place that birds may be seen in our area, or all those places that are rich in wildlife, as just about every village has its own pond, wood, or copse that attracts birds of some kind or other. In fact part of the charm of bird watching is to be able to go to one's own local patch and relax for an hour or two with no-one else around to disturb you, and to be able to escape from the world for a while. So get out and find your own corner of the country, keep a regular check on it, and record all that you see there in your note book. There is no substitute for field note taking; it will provide a picture of your patch through the seasons, and it will give pleasure when looking over your records in the future. If you see an unusual bird there then it is esesential that you take proper field notes to help you identify it correctly when you get home. If it should turn out to be a rare bird, then you will need these to send a report to the vice county recorder. [And don't forget to tell me too!] The address of the recorder for reach vice county is in the annual county report. He will appreciate an account of the birds you have seen each year on your patch, so send them in every six months.

Here is a list of some of the places that I have not had time or space to cover. Not all of them are of prime ornithological importance; in fact many are of botanical or entomological interest, but you will always see birds there. May I remind the reader once again that inclusion of a site in this book does not necessarily mean that there is unrestricted public access to a site; if you are in any doubt, then please ask the landowner first.

Cleveland:

Billingham beck valley
Seaton Sluice
Seaton Carew Church
Charlton's pond
Harrington's pond
Normansby brickworks
Marton west beck
Cow close
Hagg wood

Hartlepool Harbour and headland
Saltburn Gill
Castle Eden walkway
Bowesfield pond
Bluebell beck
Lazenby bank
Errington woods
Clarkson's wood

Yorkshire and Humberside:

The following are Yorkshire Wildlife Trust reserves. For complete details of the sites, and access arrangements, contact YWT or refer to the reserve cards which may be purchased from YWT.

North Cliffe wood: between Market Weighton and North Cave
Burton Leonard lime quarries
Pulfin Fen: north east of Beverley
Keldmarsh: in Beverley
Sherburn Willows: Sherburn in Elmett
Ashberry: near Rievaux
Little Beck wood: near Whitby
Hagg wood marsh: at Lockton near Pickering
Fordon chalk bank: 9 miles south of Scarborough
Beckhead wood: near Garrowby Hill
Wharram quarry: near Wetwang
Garbutt wood: near Sutton Bank
Hayburn Wyke: between Scarborough and Robin Hood's bay
Kipplingcotes chalk pit: near Market Weighton
Rifle Butts quarry: near Market Weighton
Fen bog: 3 miles south of Goathland
Moorlands: near Skelton
Askham bog: near York

There are a few places that can also be explored that are managed by **Humberside County Council:**

North Bank at Fimber
Bracey Bridge near Harpham
Towthorpe corner near Market Weighton
Hull-Hornsea railway line
Kelsey Hill gravel pits

These sites are under other ownership or management:

Baysgarth Park — Glanford Borough Council
Elsham Country Park — Elsham Hall
Freshney Parkway — Grimsby and Cleethorpe Councils
Donna Nook

a) Kittiwake (*Rissa tridactyla*) hanging in the upward air currents at a sea cliff.
b) Robin (*Erithacus rubecula*) the gardener's friend.
c) Fulmar (*Fulmarus glacialis*) and sea pinks.

a) Arctic skua (*Stercorarius parasiticus*) displaying to a potential mate.
b) Corncrake (*Crex crex*) at Wheldrake Ings, a very rare bird of old meadows and cornfields.
c) Waxwing (*Bombicylla garrulus*) feeding on last autumn's haws at York.

Seamer gravel pits
The Mere and Peasholme Park — Scarborough
Carlton lake
Hudson Way — disused railway track from Market Weighton to Beverley

Great northern diver, tufted duck and coot at Castle Howard.

SYSTEMATIC LIST OF BIRDS

The species list and check list do not list the birds in alphabetical order. A close look at the list will reveal that the birds are grouped into families with all the thrushes together, and all the warblers together etc. Birds fall roughly into two types, non-perching birds such as the ducks, and perching birds such as tits. The list starts with the most anatomically primitive species the divers and grebes, and progresses to the most specialised the finches and buntings. For most birdwatchers this sequence will be very familiar and easy to follow. However for those of you who find it hard to find a bird quickly there is an alphabetical index at the end that you can use.

In this list I have attempted to produce a comprehensive account of all the birds that have been seen here at least once in the last 12 years. In the case of the rarer birds, the record must have been submitted to, and accepted by, the Yorkshire Ornithologists Union. These birds are marked with the letter [R].

The birds that occur in this country are here as either breeding or non-breeding individuals. If they are breeders they fall into one of the following categories:

1. They are resident birds such as red grouse and sparrowhawk.
2. They are here as migrant birds coming to breed in the summer, such as willow warblers, redstarts etc..
3. They are semi-resident with either a few staying, or a few leaving for the winter, such as chiffchaff and black redstart.

If they are non-breeding birds then they may occur in one of the following:

1. Birds of passage returning to, or leaving, their breeding area eg. black terns.
2. Immature birds that are wandering around and are especially seen at the coast.
3. Birds spending the winter months with us that have moved south from their northern breeding ground, such as snow buntings, and redwings.

Non-breeding birds are the most unpredictable in their behaviour, as they can turn up at any time or place. They do however occur more often in spring and autumn, and it is then that birdwatchers themselves congregate at the best migration points, such as the Isles of Scilly and Fair Isle. We here in the east of the country have our own spots that regularly record exciting birds, but it is in spring and autumn that we just can never tell what is going to be in the next bush, or fly in with the next flock of waders. This list should give you a flavour of the regular birds to our area, and some of the ones that can set the pulse racing.

Recently there has been a review of the names of some of our birds in an effort to standardize them internationally, and to make the naming of them more relevant. The suggested new names, where appropriate are included after each bird in brackets.

Red-throated diver — *Gavia stellata*
Breeds in the north west of Scotland, and is the most frequently seen diver off the east coast, but is only occasionally seen on inland waters such as Scaling Dam and Tophill Low reservoirs.

Black-throated diver — *G. arctica*
Nests in smaller numbers than the last species, in similar habitats, and is recorded less often along the coast, usually as single birds.

Great northern diver — *G. immer*
Seldom recorded, but individual birds are seen most years from all coastal stations during the winter. An obliging bird stayed for a couple of weeks at Castle Howard lake in 1986.

White billed diver [R] — *G. adamsii*
A very rare bird anywhere in the country. One fed from fish scraps thrown to it by trawlermen in Hartlepool harbour in spring 1981. Another was picked up moribund after 2 days at Filey Brigg in spring 1987, and an adult in summer plumage was off Flamborough Sept. 1987.

Little grebe — *Tachybaptus ruficollis*
Found throughout the area and breeds at many suitable freshwater habitats, e.g. Broomfleet pools and Coatham Marsh.

Great crested grebe — *Podiceps cristatus*
This bird has expanded its breeding range, and consolidated within it. It is found at many gravel pits and lakes and during the winter months over 100 birds often congregate at Barmston with divers and scoters.

Red-necked grebe — *P. grisegena*
Single birds are reported regularly during the autumn and winter months at sites such as Scarborough harbour and Hornsea Mere.

Slavonian grebe — *P. auritus*
Seen less frequently along the coast than the previous species. Recorded in recent years from Tophill Low, and several other waters.

Black-necked grebe — *P. nigricolis*
This grebe nests irregularly across northern England and Scotland on inland waters. Wandering individuals often occur on waters such as Broomfleet ponds, and Hornsea Mere. Very rarely seen off the coast, but a splendid bird was in summer plumage at Scarborough harbour in 1988.

Black-browed albatross [R] — *Diomedea melanophris*
An albatross which was probably this species flew north off Filey in October 1987.

Fulmar — *Fulmarus glacialis*
Fulmars are continuing to spread southwards with further colonisations at Filey, Bempton, and Flamborough. Dark phase "blue" fulmars are also being recorded more often [Northern fulmar].

Capped petrel [R] — *Pterodroma hasitata*
A remarkable discovery of a dead capped petrel occurred on the beach at Barmston in December 1984. The first record for Yorkshire and only the second British record [Black-capped petrel].

Cory's shearwater — *Calonectris diomedea*
A Mediterranean species which is seen annually from Spurn to Teesmouth but seldom more than 10 records each year. A bird of much calmer seas than the next species.

Great shearwater — *Puffinus gravis*
This large shearwater is seen less often than the last species each autumn. Two or three records from Flamborough and Filey are about average.

Sooty shearwater — *P. griseus*
After northwesterly gales they are often seen moving north in large numbers along the coast. They breed on islands in the south Atlantic, and move north to reach our coast by mid July. After a peak around September, numbers tail off to late October.

Manx shearwater — *Puffinus puffinus puffinus*
A much smaller shearwater than the last, and is seen throughout the summer and early autumn passing along the coast, Over 1000 a day have been logged. Breeds in burrows in islands around the west of the country but not on the mainland.

Balearic/Levantine shearwater — *P. p. mauretanicus/yelkouan*
Many taxonomists regard this as a separate species. Birds showing characteristics of these Mediterranean races are being identified more regularly from coastal seawatching stations.

Little shearwater [R] — *P. assimilis*
The rarest shearwater, but single birds are recorded from most observation points each year.

Storm petrel — *Hydrobates pelagicus*
This bird is more frequently seen off the coast of Cornwall, but individual birds are reported most years [European storm-petrel].

Leech's petrel — *Oceanodroma leucorhoa*
These petrels occur off the Lancashire coast after strong n.w. gales. A bird with only one wing was found alive on the beach at Spurn in 1982 [Leach's storm-petrel].

Gannet — *Sula bassana*
Bempton cliffs is the best place in the country to see nesting gannets at close quarters, over 800 pairs bred in 1988. Gannets move large distances looking for food, and many that are seen around the east coast will be from Bass Rock [Northern gannet].

Cormorant — *Phalacrocorax carbo*
Seen fishing in a variety of waters; coastal, estuarine, harbours and often inland at Scaling Dam, Tophill Low, Wheldrake Ings etc. [Great cormorant].

Double-crested cormorant [R] — *P. auritus*
The first European record of this American species came from Charton's Pond, Teesside in spring 1989.

Shag — *P. aristotelis*
Large numbers roost on the cliffs south of Flamborough where up to 1000 roost. Much more a bird of the open seas than cormorant, but occasionally reported from inland waters.

Little bittern [R] — *Ixobrychus minutus*
Has bred in South Yorkshire recently, but this is a rare bittern seldom seen in the east. There was a male at Hornsea Mere for 2 weeks in the late spring of 1977.

Bittern — *Botaurus stellaris*
Breeds sporadically in Humberside, but there have been no confirmed breeding records recently, although single birds are often seen in the winter months [Great bittern].

Night heron [R] — *Nycticorax nycticorax*
1987 was an outstanding year for this small heron with 2 birds at Swine near Beverley, and singles at Filey and Spurn [Black-crowned night heron].

Green heron — *Butorides striatus*
An adult in a drainage dyke at Stone Creek in 1982 surprised birders looking for a Great white egret! This was the first British record of this American bird since one was shot in Cornwall in 1889 [Green-backed heron].

Cattle egret — *Bubulcus ibis*
Another rare egret, which as its name suggests usually associates with cattle. One near Riveaux Abbey 1981 and another at Hornsea Mere 1986.

Great white egret [R] — *Egretta alba*
One at Stone Creek in 1982 [Great egret].

Little egret [R] — *Egretta garzetta*
One at Seamer G.P. June 1984, and one at Coatham Marsh April 1986.

Squacco heron [R] — *Ardeola ralloides*
A rare bird even in Europe. One stayed for 2 weeks at Easington in late spring 1979.

Grey heron — *Ardea cinerea*
There are several heronries in the area such as at Kirkdale, Crathorne, and down the lower Derwent. Immature birds and non-breeders may be encountered throughout the year at any gravel pit, river or water meadow.

Purple heron [R] — *A. purpurea*
Breeds in isolated areas throughout Europe and occurs here only occasionally. Singles at Seamer G.P. May 1981, and Filey Dams May 1987, are the most recent. Despite its size it can easily go undetected.

White stork — *Ciconia ciconia*
A conspicuous bird which is being reintroduced into Holland, so birds seen on the east coast may be of Dutch origin. One at Hornsea Mere October 1983.

Spoonbill — *Platalea leucorodia*
A stocky bird which breeds successfully in Holland and wandering birds are often seen in Norfolk. A long stayer spent the summer at Blacktoft Sands 1987. There many other records from Spurn and Flamborough etc. [White spoonbill].

Mute swan — *Cygnus olor*
Widely distributed across the area with a wintering flock of over 150 birds most years at Hornsea Mere. Declining numbers in some areas are doubtless due to lead poisoning and disturbance at the nest. A sad record is of 9 dead along Pocklington Canal in the early part of 1982.

Bewick's swan — *C. columbianus*
The river Derwent is the best place to see this Siberian swan. Over 200 birds have wintered there in recent years, around Ellerton and Aughton.

Whooper swan — *C. cygnus*
Much more widely distributed than the last species, but usually seen in smaller numbers. The lower Derwent is again a favoured area, but birds often turn up at many open waters and flooded fields.

Bean goose — *Anser fabalis*
Small numbers of birds winter in the area at places such as Tophill Low and Cowpen Marsh.

Pink-footed goose — *A. brachyrhyncus*
Winter numbers on the Humber build up from October to sizeable flocks of up to 1600 in good years. Birds move around the estuary and may be seen from Whitton Sands or Blacktoft Sands.

White-fronted goose — *A. albifrons*
Single birds from north Russia are seen each winter at widely scattered sites such as Coatham and Cowpen Marshes, Spurn etc. Most records are of the nominate race, but the Greenland race *A. a. flavirostris* is also reported.

Lesser white-fronted goose [R] — *A. erythropus*
Despite breeding in Lapland this goose is seen less frequently than the last species as it migrates southwards towards Greece. One at Hornsea Mere in spring 1977 and another at Broomfleet May 1986.

Greylag goose — *A. anser*
Many pairs of feral birds breed throughout the area and large flocks collect at Crookfoot Res., Castle Howard, Hornsea Mere etc.

Snow goose — *A. caerulescens*
It is difficult to assess whether any of the birds seen have made an Atlantic crossing as small numbers breed in the Scottish Isles.

Canada goose — *Branta canadensis*
Introduced to the U.K. in the 17th century and now a familiar bird throughout the area.

Barnacle goose — *B. leucopsis*
Whilst most records refer to feral birds, some of wild origin are recorded each winter. Up to 80 were at Hornsea Mere in 1984 and 130 at Castle Howard.

Brent goose — *B. bernicla*
A coastal goose seen on the mud flats of the Humber and Teesmouth, but smaller numbers occur all along the coast in winter. Numbers have increased over the past 10 years.

Red-breasted goose [R] — *B. ruficollis*
A rare visitor to the east coast that usually associates with Brent or White-fronted geese. One at Spurn in 1978 and another at Barmston in 1984.

Egyptian goose — *Alopochen aegyptiacus*
Feral birds breed widely along Norfolk coast, so records from our area could be wandering British birds, rather than escapes.

Ruddy shelduck — *Tadorna ferruginea*
Although recorded most years, genuine vagrancy is not supported by European records. A pair with a young bird on Whitton Sands in 1978 had probably nested locally. Another at Teesmouth in 1988.

Shelduck — *T. tadorna*
Breeds in many suitable areas such as the Derwent Valley and Seal Sands. Peak numbers of over 2000 have been recorded on the Humber and over 1000 at Teesmouth.

Wigeon — *Anas penelope*
They breed at several sites in the area but vast numbers occur on the Lower Derwent in winter.

Pintail — *A. acuta*
Seldom reported as more than the occasional bird at Teesmouth, but 100+ are often seen on the Humber such as at Cherry Cob sands. Many spend the winter on the Lower Derwent [Northern Pintail].

Teal — *A. crecca*
A few pairs breed along the Lower Derwent, but they occur in vast

numbers in winter with flocks of up to 2000 reported [Green-winged teal].

Garganey — *A. Querquedula*
Probably breed in several localities, and appear all over the area especially at Blacktoft, Filey Dams, and Haverton Hole.

Blue-winged teal [R] — *A. discors*
This pretty teal is a very rare American visitor; one at Coatham Marsh in Autumn 87.

Shoveller — *A. clypeata*
Breeds at Blacktoft Sands and several other places; autumn numbers increase to give 100+ at Tophill Low, and Hornsea Mere [Northern Shoveller].

Mallard — *A. platyrhynchos*
A common and familiar bird of all ponds, lakes and rivers.

Gadwall — *A. strepera*
Small numbers occur at most sites throughout the year, but Hornsea Mere has a large winter population.

Pochard — *Aythya ferina*
Breeds all over the east of the country in suitable habitat such as at Tophill Low and occasionally at Teesside. Over 2000 winter on the Lower Derwent [Common Pochard].

Ring-necked duck [R] — *A. collaris*
This used to be a very rare American vagrant, but it is now recorded annually. The drake bird at Tophill Low returned for several winters in succession.

Tufted duck — *A. fuligula*
This species was first recorded breeding in Britain in Yorkshire in 1849, but has since colonised just about every county, and is a familiar bird on all waters.

Scaup — *A. marila*
Most regularly recorded in flight off the coast, but they are hard to identify. Single birds turn up in cold weather especially on the lagoons at Easington, and at Hornsea Mere [Greater Scaup].

Eider — *Somateria mollissima*
They can be seen feeding and diving for mussels all along the coast where there are suitable beds [Common Eider].

Long-tailed duck — *Clangula hyemalis*
Seen in the winter as single birds sheltering in bays such as at Filey or at Hornsea.

Common scoter — *Melanitta nigra*
Large flocks can be seen all along the coast of Bridlington bay. Small parties turn up on inland waters each year [Black Scoter].

Surf scoter [R] — *M. perspicillata*
One at Filey in '82, and another flew past Flamborough in '83.

Velvet scoter — *M. fusca*
Seen in flight regularly each autumn from Filey Brigg and Flamborough, and amongst rafts of common scoter in Bridlington Bay.

Goldeneye — *Bucephala clangula*
Occurs at all inland waters from July onwards. Large numbers may be seen at Seal Sands in mid-winter [Common Goldeneye].

Barrow's goldeneye [R] — *B. islandica*
An immature female was at Wheldrake Ings autumn '87, but not officially on the British list yet.

Smew — *Mergus albellus*
There are few prettier birds than male smew, but most birds that occur here are females or immature males. The winter of '84/85 was an exception with many being seen all over the east of the country.

Red-breasted merganser — *M. serrator*
Small numbers are seen each month along the coast such as at Filey Bay and at Cornelian Bay.

Goosander — *M. Merganser*
As this bird breeds along fast running waters such as the river Wharfe, it is not surprising that it should be seen so often on inland waters such as Hornsea Mere and Scaling Dam each winter.

Ruddy duck — *Oxyura jamaicensis*
These birds were imported from North America in 1948 and allowed to breed freely at Slimbridge. Some young escaped, and the feral population has now started to breed in Yorkshire with wandering birds seen all over the county.

Honey Buzzard — *Pernis aviporus*
Single birds are reported each spring passage [Western Honey-buzzard].

Red kite — *Milvus milvus*
Seen most years, but birds seen on the east of the country are unlikely to be wandering Welsh birds.

Black kite [R] — *M. migrans*
A former great rarity, which is being recorded more often probably because of range expansion. One was seen perched on a fence post at Spurn in '85.

White-tailed eagle [R] — *Haliaeetus albicilla*
An immature bird was at Thorne moors in '82, and would be a continental vagrant. Another at Blacktoft Sands and Filey in '85.

Marsh harrier — *Circus aeruginosus*
Many more are being seen each year; breeds periodically at Blacktoft Sands.

Hen harrier — *C. cyaneus*
They are best seen in the winter at one of the roosts at Blacktoft, Thorne Moors, Scaling Dam, or Fylingdales.

Montagu's harrier — *C. Pygargus*
Fortunately these birds are breeding much more successfully in cereal fields down south, so there are more records in recent years of northern vagrancy.

Goshawk — *Accipiter gentilis*
This magnificent hawk would rapidly re-colonise many parts of the country were it not for continued persecution by the mindless minority of egg collectors and uninformed keepers that still persist. Several records each year from all parts of the area [Northern Goshawk].

Sparrowhawk — *A. nisus*
Since stricter controls have been placed on the use and abuse of pesticides this bird has made a welcome comeback to most woods [Northern Sparrowhawk].

Buzzard — *Buteo buteo*
Single birds can turn up at just about any part of the country, particularly on the coast and the wolds [Common Buzzard].

Rough-legged buzzard — *B. lagopus*
The best place to see them is at Bransdale in the early part of the year; but be patient, this is a vast area, and they are not easy to find. One near Sledmere in '89.

Golden eagle — *Aquila Chrysaetos*
Very rarely recorded in our area, but juveniles are often seen at Gouthwaite reservoir in winter.

Osprey — *Pandion haliaetus*
Seen each passage, with some birds stopping over in springtime. May one day nest in Yorkshire!

Lesser kestrel — *Falco naumanni*
A very rare falcon in the county. One at Atwick in '83, was the first since a male bird was seen at Fairburn in '79.

Kestrel — *F. tinnunculus*
A familiar bird breeding all over the county, and seen especially hovering at the side of roads [Common Kestrel].

Red-footed falcon [R] — *F. vespertinus*
This dainty falcon is being seen more often. A male bird stayed for several weeks at Blacktoft Sands in '87.

Kestrel.

Merlin — *F. columbarius*
Seen along the coast in the winter months such as at Barmston and Spurn, and North Tees marshes. Breeds on suitable moors, but has declined in recent years.

Hobby — *F. subbuteo*
A fast flying bird that feeds on insects as much as on other birds; seen infrequently all over the area, but breeds in the south of the county [Northern Hobby].

Gyr falcon [R] — *F. rusticolus*
The most powerful of the falcons; a massive bird the size of a buzzard, but only seen in Autumn '83 at Spurn in the past 10 years.

Eleonora's falcon [R] — *F. Eleonorae*
A remarkable record of one found dead in a vegetable plot at Patrington in '81 was only the second British record of this Mediterranean raptor.

Peregrine falcon — *F. peregrinus*
Fortunately these birds are being sighted more regularly, and with regular breeding at an eyrie near the M62 it is hopeful that it will not be long before they return fully to suitable sites along the east coast, and the North York Moors.

Red grouse — *Lagopus lagopus*
There are a lot of birds on the North York Moors, but numbers have declined recently, probably due to over-shooting and a reduction in the amount of heather on the moor, which provides most of their food.

Grey partridge — *Perdix perdix*
A widely distributed bird, but it again has suffered losses in recent years due to the removal of hedgerows, and an increased use of pesticides which reduce the numbers of aphids available for the chicks to feed on.

Red-legged partridge — *Alectoris rufa*
Much the most frequently seen partridge to the east of the A1. They were originally introduced to this country in 1673, and have adapted well. Some misguided people have recently been releasing chukars, and these can successfully breed with red-legged.

Quail — *Coturnix coturnix*
A secretive bird that breeds most years along the Lower Derwent, but is seldom seen [Common Quail].

Pheasant — *Phasianus colchicus*
A familiar bird in the countryside, but again not native to this country. Albino and melanistic birds are regularly seen.

Water rail — *Rallus aquaticus*
Probably much more widely distributed than records suggest, as it is a shy bird most of the year, but becomes confiding in hard weather. Breeds in most wetland and marshy areas.

Spotted crake — *Porzana porzana*
These birds seem to turn up every year at Long Drag, Tophill Low, and Blacktoft Sands. A calling male was heard at Fulford Ings near York in '84.

Corncrake — *Crex crex*
There used to be corncrake calling from every hay meadow in the land before the advent of mechanised harvesting. Nowadays the hay is cut for silage earlier and there is little chance for the young to escape. A pair probably nested at Wheldrake in '87, but they are a very rare bird now [Corn Crake].

Moorhen — *Gallinula chloropus*
A widespread bird of water margins that is found all over the county. Numbers seem to be declining in some areas, and this may be due to an increase in the numbers of mink around [Common Moorhen].

Coot — *Fulica atra*
A familiar and gregarious bird of all inland waters, with 2000+ at Hornsea Mere [Black Coot].

Crane — *Grus grus*
An elegant bird of open countryside; three birds were in the Bubwith area in May '86, and singles are reported every year from around the county.

Oystercatcher — *Haematopus ostralegus*
Breeds along Pocklington canal in small numbers, but is very numerous along the entire coastline as birds move to their wintering quarters from July onwards [Northern Pied Oystercatcher].

Black-winged stilt [R] — *Himantopus himantopus*
A common European bird that nested in Norfolk in '87, and a pair mated at Blacktoft Sands in '83. One at Coatham marsh May '86.

Avocet — *Recurvirostra revosetta*
This bird is the emblem of the RSPB and is one of the many success stories that they can boast of. There are several breeding areas in Norfolk now, so it is not surprising that the odd potential coloniser should be seen in our area [Pied Avocet].

Collared pratincole [R] — *Glareola pratincola*
One flew south over Spurn in '82.

Stone-curlew — *Bhurinus oedicnemus*
One at Wheldrake in '84. Quite an unexpected bird to find here [Northern Thick-knee].

Little ringed plover — *Charadrius dubius*
This is another recent coloniser, and only nested in Britain in 1938. Since then they have spread successfully throughout our area, and are often found around gravel pits.

Ringed plover — *C. hiaticula*
Seen throughout the year, with numbers rising to a peak in May as birds of the race 'tundrae' move north to their breeding grounds.

Kentish plover — *C. alexandrinus*
Kentish plovers bred in Lincolnshire in the early '80's and there are single birds seen in springtime most years.

Greater sand plover [R] — *C. leschenaultii*
One at Spurn in summer '81 was the first Yorkshire record.

Dotterel — *Eudromias morinellus*
Seen in trips in May at Rosedale and Goole Fields, and single birds are seen most autumns along the coast [Mountain Dotterel].

Pacific golden plover [R] — *Pluvialis fulva*
Now considered to be a separate species from the next; one at Fraisthorpe in '85, and one at Flamborough in '86.

American golden plover [R] — *P. dominica*
A full summer plumage bird was at Sammy's Point, Spurn in '84. Another at Saltholme in autumn '88.

Golden plover — *P. apricaria*
Breed on the North York Moors, and flocks several thousand strong then gather each autumn in low lying areas such as Cherry Cobb, Lower Derwent, and Teesside Airport [European Golden Plover].

Grey plover — *P. squatarola*
Unlike the previous species they do not breed in this country, but occur on passage along the coast.

Lapwing — *Vanellus vanellus*
Intensification of agriculture has led to a reduction in breeding numbers on the Wolds, but they are still a familiar bird to all country people [Northern Lapwing].

Turnstone — *Arenaria interpres*
Non-breeders are seen all along the coast throughout the year [Ruddy turnstone].

Knot — *Calidris canutus*
Estuary numbers can be very impressive, with up to 10,000 at high tide roosts on the Humber and 6,000 on Teesmouth [Red Knot].

Sanderling — *C. alba*
It is always a pleasure to see these birds running along the sea edge in winter. In spring they take on a very attractive ruddy plumage before they go back to the north.

Long-toed stint [R] — *C. subminuta*
The first British record was at Haverton Hole, North Tees in '82.

Red-necked stint [R] — *C. ruficollis*
The first confirmed record for Britain at Blacktoft Sands in '86 was the subject of some local argument as to its identity before common sense prevailed [Rufous-necked Stint].

Little stint — *C. minuta*
Seen every year in small numbers at Long Drag, Easington lagoons, Blacktoft Sands, and many other places on passage.

Temminck's stint — *C. temminckii*
Scarcer than the previous species, and seen mainly in May. A few pairs nest in Scotland.

Semi-palmated sandpiper [R] — *C. pusilla*
One at Beacon Land ponds in '85 (for one afternoon) and one at Saltholme in may 89 are the only records of this very rare American wader.

White-rumped sandpiper [R] — *C. fuscicollis*
There is usually about one record per year from places such as Long Drag, Blacktoft Sands etc.

Baird's sandpiper [R] — *C. bairdii*
Rarer than the previous species to which it bears a superficial resemblance. One at Long Drag in '86.

Pectoral sandpiper — *C. melanotos*
This is the most common of the American waders to turn up here, and is reported every year from coastal wetlands.

Sharp-tailed sandpiper [R] — *C. acuminata*
This resembles the previous species, but is much rarer. One at Flamborough in '83.

Curlew sandpiper — *C. ferruginea*
An elegant wader that turns up most frequently in autumn and is found along inland waters as well as estuaries in small numbers.

Purple sandpiper — *C. maritima*
A very tame bird that can be seen throughout the winter along any stretch of the coast where there are rocks and racks.

Dunlin — *C. alpina*
The most familiar of our coastal waders, they are found along all types of shore and estuary at all times of the year. Humber counts have exceeded 20,000 in January.

Broad-billed sandpiper [R] — *Limicola falcinellus*
These birds are being identified more often in May, as stragglers join ringed plovers migrating north. Seen at Hull docks and Long Drag in '86 and at Blacktoft Sands in '88.

Ruff — *Pilomachus pugnax*
Greatham Creek is a good place to see ruff, as also is Blacktoft Sands at high tides in August. Some birds summer in the lower river meadows.

Buff-breasted sandpiper [R] — *Tryngites subraficellis*
Being seen less frequently in the area; one at Long Drag in '87.

Jack snipe — *Lymnocryptes minimus*
Single birds are usually only seen when flushed accidentally, so the true numbers that winter here must be higher than reports suggest.

Snipe — *Gallinago gallinago*
Breeds on moorlands and on lower marshlands. In winter many sites hold over 100 birds such as Thornton marsh [Common Snipe].

Great snipe [R] — *G. media*
One at Flamborough in '84.

Long-billed dowitcher [R] — *Limnodromus scolopaceus*
Another rare US wanderer, one at Filey in '85.

Woodcock — *Scolopax rusticola*
Seen roding in summer evenings wherever there is mature deciduous woodland. Some birds move to the coast in autumn [Eurasian Woodcock].

Black-tailed godwit — *Limosa limosa*
Are breeding once again in East Anglia, and regularly occur on the North Tees Marshes as well as Blacktoft Sands and Wheldrake Ings.

Bar-tailed godwit — *L. lapponica*
Highest concentrations occur in winter at Teesmouth, with smaller numbers on the Humber at Cherry Cobb etc.

Hudsonian godwit [R] — *L. haemastica*
This is a very scarce bird even in North America, yet one occurred at Blacktoft in '82 and what was probably the same bird, again in '83.

Whimbrel — *Numenius phaeopus*
Large number of whimbrel pass south through Teesmouth, Flamborough and Spurn each autumn.

Curlew — *N. arquata*
Breeds on both upland moors, and on lowland marshes; they congregate along the coast in autumn with peaks of 500+ at Teesmouth, and 1000+ on the Humber [Western Curlew].

Spotted redshank — *Tringa erythropus*
Occur in small numbers on freshwater margins from spring to late autumn.

Redshank — *T. totanus*
A familiar bird, breeding along the Lower Derwent, and congregating in large numbers on the Tees and Humber in winter [Common Redshank].

Greenshank — *T. nebularia*
A few birds breed in Scotland, and in autumn numbers are swollen by continental birds that are returning south. Seen on many lakes and marshes [Common Greenshank].

Lesser yellowlegs [R] — *T. flavipes*
One at Flamborough in '78, and another at Filey Dams in '86.

Green sandpiper — *T. ochropus*
Over-winters along Pocklington Canal, and many sites, such as Tophill Low, have over 10 in autumn.

Hooded crow, bar-tailed godwits and dunlins at Spurn.

Wood sandpiper — *T. glareola*
Never as frequently seen as the last species with single birds at places such as Spurn and Greatham Creek most years.

Common sandpiper — *Actitis hypoleucos*
Breeds along rivers up in the Dales, and occurs in small numbers at Hornsea Mere and Seamer Road Mere on passage.

Spotted sandpiper [R] — *A. macularia*
A rare American cousin of the last species, the first Yorkshire record is of one killed at Whitby in 1849.

Grey phalarope — *Phalaropus fulicarius*
Seen at Filey Brigg, and in flight from Flamborough most winters.

Red-necked phalarope — *P. lobatus*
Three together at Tophill Low D reservoir when it was being drained in '86 were a fine sight.

Wilson's Phalarope [R] — *P. tricolor*
Dorman's pool has had more than its fair share of this rarity with single birds nearly every autumn in the late '70's. One at Blacktoft Sands in '83.

Pomarine skua — *Stercorarius pomarinus*
Recorded each autumn from all coastal stations, but some years such as '85 can produce unprecedented numbers with birds turning up far inland.

Arctic skua — *S. parasiticus*
This is the most frequently seen of the skuas and over 500 have been seen in a day from Scarborough Marine Drive in autumn.

Long-tailed skua — *S. longicaudus*
The rarest and most graceful of the genus. '88 was the year that produced up to 20 per day past some sea watching points.

Great skua — *S. skua*
Most birdwatchers call them bonxies. They are magnificent, powerful flyers and are seen all along the coast, with peak passage in August and September.

Mediterranean gull — *Larus melanocephalus*
Being reported more frequently as birdwatchers take a greater interest in gulls; long stayers could often be seen throughout the year at Bridlington harbour and another at Hornsea Mere.

Laughing gull [R] — *L. atricilla*
One could often be seen on the goal posts at a playing field in Hull in '84. A rare US visitor.

Little gull — *L. minutus*
Seen daily along the coast, often in large numbers past Hornsea in autumn.

Sabine's gull — *L. sabini*
Regarded by many as the most attractive of the gulls. Seen in autumn after strong north-westerly winds from Flamborough and Filey.

Bonaparte's gull [R] — *L. philadelphia*
One at Saltholme in '77 stayed for 6 weeks.

Black-headed gull — *L. ridibundus*
Breeds on lowland water meadows such as near Bubwith Ings, and often roosts in vast numbers at sea and on inland waters.

Common gull — *L. canus*
The gull of the school playing field; not as common as the last species, but again roosts in large flocks [Mew Gull].

Ring-billed gull [R] — *L. delawarensis*
The first for Britain was only seen in 1973, but so many are now seen in the west of the country that they are not now considered a rarity! However they are here; one at Whitton Sands in '81.

Lesser black-backed gull — *L. fuscus*
Mainly a summer visitor, and can be seen in several places such as Blacktoft Sands in large flocks at roost.

Herring gull — *L. argentatus*
This is the typical 'sea' gull. It is found scavenging for food at resorts, and breeds along cliff tops, and even the roofs of houses.

Iceland Gull — *L. glaucoides*
Not as commonly seen as the next species, but occurs each winter in small numbers along the coast.

Glaucous gull — *L. hyperboreus*
A more powerful and aggressive gull than the last, often seen accompanying fishing boats home to harbour in winter, or searching for food on rubbish tips.

Great black-backed gull — *L. marinus*
A massive, long lived gull that can fly great distances at sea with little effort. Seen just about everywhere.

Ross's gull [R] — *Rhodostethia rosea*
Filey Brigg has twice played host to this tiny gull from north west arctic, in '80 and '83. Further records came from Hornsea and Flamborough in '86.

Kittiwake — *Rissa tridactyla*
There are vast numbers along the east coast with colonies wherever there are good cliffs [Black-legged Kittiwake].

Ivory gull [R] — *Pagophila eburnea*
A gull of the arctic pack ice; a juvenile in '83 should have been more at home at Spitzbergen than at Saltburn.

Gull-billed tern [R] — *Gelochelidon nilotica*
An extremely rare tern seen occasionally from Flamborough Head.

Caspian tern [R] — *Sterna caspia*
Another tern seen occasionally at Flamborough; and one at Filey in '82.

Sandwich tern — *S. sandvicensis*
A summer visitor, and is seen on passage all along the coast; birds breed on the Farne Islands and Coquette.

Roseate tern — *S. dougallii*
The scarcest of a trio of terns of this genus, and is seen less frequently each year off the east coast. A few pairs nest on Coquette.

Common tern — *S. hirundo*
Breeds on some inland waters, and occurs on passage in reasonably large numbers each year.

Arctic tern — *S. paradisaea*
Superficially similar to the previous species; breeds on the Farne Isles and feeding parties are seen throughout the summer and autumn along the coast.

Little tern — *S. albifrons*
A dainty tern that tries to nest each year at Easington but at South Gare, where they are protected, they are doing well.

Whiskered tern [R] — *Chlidonias hybridus*
Breeds in the Carmargue, so one at Castle Howard Lake in '83 was a long way from home.

Black tern — *C. niger*
Seen in small groups in springtime at inland waters such as Tophill Low, and on passage along the coast as single birds throughout the summer months.

White-winged black tern [R] — *C. leucopterus*
Seen at Hull Docks in '86, and another flew north over Spurn in '83.

Guillemot — *Uria aalge*
Nest in large colonies along the chalk sea cliffs, and often pass along the coast at 1000 per hour [Common Guillemot].

Razorbill — *Alca torda*
There are much smaller numbers than the previous species, but they can always be seen along the ledges at Bempton in Spring competing for nesting space.

Black guillemot — *Cepphus grylle*
Plentiful off rocky Scottish beaches; seen only occasionally as single birds in winter at Filey Bay.

Little auk — *Alle alle*
A tiny bird that nests on arctic islands in colonies a million strong. Storm driven to our shores, many die of starvation in winter.

Puffin — *Fratercula arctica*
A favourite bird of many people, they can be seen well from the viewing areas at Bempton each summer [Atlantic Puffin].

Rock dove — *Columba livia*
The species' gene pool is being diluted by breeding with the huge flocks of feral pigeons that get lost along the coast. Flamborough Head is about as far south as the pure birds range [Rock Pigeon].

Stock dove — *C. oenas*
Seen in pairs throughout the countryside each summer, and in small flocks in winter [Stock Pigeon].

Woodpigeon — *C. palumbus*
Shooting these birds has no effect on their numbers; they simply move on to the next field. Flocks of 10,000 strong have been seen near Hornsea [Common Wood Pigeon].

Collared dove — *Streptopelia decaocto*
Unknown in the UK until 1952, when the first was seen in Lincolnshire. Birds nested in Norfolk in '56, and have now almost become a pest in some areas. A delightful garden bird.

Turtle dove — *S. turtur*
A summer visitor found in most woodlands on the east, but may be declining slightly in the Wolds.

Cuckoo — *Cuculus canorus*
Seen throughout the area from April to August. A common bird along the Lower Derwent and in the Wolds [Common Cuckoo].

Great spotted cuckoo [R] — *Clamator glandarius*
A juvenile along the Humber near spurn in '82.

Yellow-billed cuckoo [R] — *Coccyzus americanus*
One ringed at Spurn in '78. Regrettably these American birds usually die shortly after reaching this country.

Barn Owl — *Tyto alba*
Declining in many areas, but is still relatively common in the vale of York, and Holderness.

Ring ouzel.

Little owl — *Athene noctua*
Was introduced to this country in the last century, and has adapted to conditions here without competing with native birds. Breeds in various habitats from orchards to moors.

Tawny owl — *Strix aluco*
A common owl, frequently heard in towns at night.

Long-eared owl — *Asio otus*
One of the few birds that have benefited from afforestation of low lying areas, and breeds at several sites in the Wolds. Each winter Continental birds arrive on the east, and often roost communally.

Short-eared owl — *Asio flammeus*
Nests at several Humber sites, and is often seen along the coast during the day hunting. There were 13 at Greatham Creek in autumn '86.

Tengmalm's owl [R] — *Aegolius funereus*
The emblem of the Spurn owl appreciation society! One there for 2 weeks in spring '83.

Nightjar — *Caprimulgus europaeus*
Declining nationally due to loss of habitat, but still survives at Hatfield Moor, Strensall, and Skipwith commons [European Nightjar].

Swift — *Apus apus*
Widely distributed and often common in towns [Common Swift].

Alpine swift [R] — *Apus melba*
One at Bempton in '88 for 2 days.

Kingfisher — *Arcedo atthis*
Suffers considerable losses in numbers in hard winters, but is increasing all over the area at present [River Kingfisher].

Bee-eater [R] — *Merops apiaster*
Three birds were well observed at Pickering in August '87 [European Bee-eater].

Hoopoe — *Upupa epops*
Another splendid continental beauty, a long stayer at Hull in '87, and one at Whitby in '83. Several other records exist recently.

Wryneck — *Jynx torquilla*
Seen every autumnal passage from Hartlepool Headland to Spurn.

Green woodpecker — *Picus viridis*
Spreading slowly northwards, but these birds are heard more often than they are seen. They frequent plantations and deciduous woods.

Great spotted woodpecker — *Dendrocopos major*
Common throughout the area with obliging individuals in the Forge Valley area. Some continental arrivals in autumn.

Lesser spotted woodpecker — *D. minor*
Very much scarcer than the last species with several pairs in the York to Helmsley area.

Short-toed lark [R] — *Calandrella brachydactyla*
One at Aldbrough early winter '87.

Woodlark — *Lullula arborea*
The occasional bird turns up along the coast each autumn, but they are much nicer to see in their breeding grounds in the Breckands of East Anglia [Wood Lark].

Skylark — *Alauda arvensis*
A hot summer day is not complete without a skylark singing way up in the air. Large flocks gather in the winter, often over 300 strong [Sky Lark].

Shore lark — *Eremophila alpestris*
Seen in very small numbers along Bridlington Bay each winter. Barmston is a favoured spot [Horned Lark].

Sand Martin — *Riparia riparia*
Suffered a calamatous fall in numbers in '86 due to poor conditions in their wintering quarters; many colonies were empty as a result. Numbers have recovered somewhat since.

Swallow — *Hirundo rustica*
Seen all over the country from April to the return passage in September when large numbers move south. Some inland roosts number over 100,000 birds [Barn Swallow].

Red-rumped swallow [R] — *H. daurica*
A scarce European vagrant; several sightings in the autumn of '87 along the coast were exceptional.

House martin — *Delchion urbica*
A familiar associate of man, but some birds continue to nest on traditional cliff faces such as at Flamborough Head.

Richard's pipit — *Anthus novaeseelandiae*
Single birds are recorded most years at Teesmouth, Spurn and Flamborough.

Tawny pipit — *A. campestris*
Seen much less frequently than the last species; one at Hull docks in '85.

Olive-backed pipit [R] — *A. hodgsoni*
A true rarity, but is being identified more often, with birds at Spurn in '87 and '88, and Filey in '87.

Tree pipit — *A. trivialis*
Seen in immature deciduous woodland all over the county.

Meadow pipit — *A pratensis*
A typical bird of meadows, moors, and Wolds valleys. Flocks several thousand strong can move along the coast in Autumn.

Red-throated pipit [R] — *A. cervinus*
One at Filey in spring '85.

Rock pipit — *A spinoleta*
Found all along rocky parts of the coast and at harbours throughout the year.

Water pipit — *A spinoleta*
Single birds are recorded each year in spring and autumn.

Yellow wagtail — *Motacilla flava*
An attractive summer visitor; occasionally the continental race, blue-headed wagtail, is also seen.

Grey wagtail — *M. cinerea*
A common bird of fast flowing streams such as at Thornton Dale, and on North York Moors.

Pied wagtails.

Pied wagtail — *M. alba*
The most familiar of the genus, they roost in large numbers in winter. Birds of the northern race, white wagtail are frequent in spring at Spurn.

Waxwing — *Bombicylla garrulus*
The best place to see waxwings is usually the old railway track at Guisborough, but they may occur in an urban garden anywhere feeding on cotoneaster berries. Large numbers occurred in autumn '88, with over 400 in Teesside alone [Bohemian Waxwing].

Dipper — *Cinclus cinclus*
Common in the Dales, but very few pairs in the east of the county [White-throated Dipper].

Wren — *Troglodytes troglodytes*
One of our most common birds especially in scrubby woodland [Northern Wren].

Dunnock — *Prunella modularis*
A common garden and hedgerow bird [Hedge Accentor].

Robin — *Erithacus rubecula*
A familiar and friendly garden bird; large numbers of immigrants come into the country in autumn [European Robin].

Thrush nightingale [R] — *Luscinia luscinia*
Very similar to nightingale, with a few breast speckles. Very difficult to observe, as it is a persistant skulker. Occasionally seen at Spurn.

Nightingale — *L. megarhynchos*
Well known as a superb songster; a few pairs at Thorne Moors each year [Common Nightingale].

Bluethroat — *L. svecica*
Turns up mainly in springtime in Flamborough, South Gare etc; early arrivals tend to be of the white spotted race, and later birds are of the red spotted race.

Black redstart — *Phoenicurus ochruros*
They prefer untidy derelict concreted areas, and breed in industrial sites in large towns. Migrant birds occur regularly along the coast in spring and autumn.

Redstart — *P. phoenicurus*
One of the most attractive of woodland birds, they are plentiful on the wolds and eastern woodlands [Common Redstart].

Whinchat — *Saxicola rubetra*
Nest on Wolds valleys, and move in good numbers along the coast in August and September.

Stonechat — *S. torquata*
A frequent bird in the west of the country, but much scarcer over here with single birds each year at Teesmouth, and occasionally birds of the Siberian race at Spurn [Common Stonechat].

Wheatear — *Oenanthe oenanthe*
Breeds on the North Yorks Moors, and are seen widely on passage each year [Northern Wheatear].

Rock thrush [R] — *Monticola saxatilis*
One caught and ringed at Spurn in '84.

Ring Ouzel — *Turdus torquatus*
Breeds on the North Yorks Moors, and are often flushed from bushes in autumn at the coast.

Blackbird — *T. merula*
A common garden bird, with large numbers swelling the British population each autumn from Scandinavia.

Eye-browed thrush [R] — *T. obscurus*
One at Aldbrough in '81 was the first for the county [Eyebrowed Thrush].

Fieldfare — *T. pilaris*
Large flocks are often seen and heard chattering across the sky as they move inland after arriving in autumn.

Song thrush — *T. philomelos*
A partial migrant with much smaller numbers involved than with the last species.

Redwing — *T. iliacus*
More susceptible to severe conditions than other large thrushes, and often become very tame in hard frosts. They scavenge hedges along with fieldfare and blackbirds for berries.

Mistle thrush — *T. viscivorus*
A large and often aggressive resident, fond of playing fields and orchards.

Cetti's warbler — *Cettia cetti*
A recent coloniser to southern reedbeds; one at Spurn in '88.

Grasshopper warbler — *Locustella naevia*
A marshland skulker that can often sing in the open, but be very hard to pick out because of its ventriloquial reeling. Breeds regularly at Carlton Marsh, and Thornton Marsh.

River warbler [R] — *L. fluviatilis*
The first county record was of one at Spurn in '81 in a year when there were several other records in the country.

Savi's warbler [R] — *L. luscinioides*
Another recent coloniser in East Anglia, one at Spurn in '84.

Aquatic warbler [R] — *Acrocephalus paludicola*
A rare warbler, one at Long Drag in '86. Care is needed with identification, as the inexperienced observer could be enthused by a young sedge warbler.

Sedge warbler — *A. schoenobaenus*
Common in hedgerows and bushes near marshlands in summer.

Blyth's reed warbler [R] — *A. dumentorum*
One caught and ringed in sea buckthorn at Spurn in '84, another at Flamborough in '86.

Marsh warbler — *A. palustris*
A few pairs breed in Midland counties; trapped at Spurn occasionally.

Reed warbler — *A scirpaceus*
They prefer much wetter areas than sedge warblers, and are plentiful at Blacktoft Sands.

Great reed warbler [R] — *A. arundinaceus*
One at Blacktoft in '87, and another at Saltmarsh Delft in '84.

Icterine warbler — *Hippolais icterina*
Several birds are recorded each autumn along the coast.

Melodious warbler — *H. polyglotta*
Very similar to the previous species, but much the scarcer of the two. One at Flamborough in '83.

Booted warbler [R] — *H. caligata*
Another very rare warbler that has been seen at Spurn. One in '81.

Desert warbler [R] — *Sylvia nana*
It was Flamborough that had this rarity in '81, a remarkable year!

Subalpine warbler [R] — *S. cantillans*
Very rare, but recorded at Spurn in '85 and '86.

Sardinian warbler [R] — *S. melancephala*
A very common bird of the Mediterranean, but one at Spurn in '82 was the first for the county.

Barred warbler — *S. nisoria*
Seen every year on the east, but despite what the field guides say, in autumn you will not see bars on these birds.

Lesser whitethroat — *S. curruca*
Another species that has suffered a reduction in pairs due to a drought in the Sahel region of the Sahara. They have recovered their numbers recently.

Whitethroat — *S. communis*
Much the more common of the two congeners, and very obvious in song flight over hawthorn scrub [Common Whitethroat].

Garden warbler — *S. borin*
Not really a garden bird, but commonly seen in woodland as its Linnaean name suggests.

Blackcap — *S. atricapilla*
Only the male has a black cap, the females and juveniles are chestnut red. Frequent in woods.

Pallas's warbler [R] — *Phylloscopus proregulus*
Many superlatives have been used to describe this once ultra-rare Siberian vagrant. They are being seen most years at Flamborough and Spurn now.

Yellow-browed warbler — *P. inornatus*
Seen at Scarborough, Locke Park, Filey Dams etc. most autumns.

Greenish warbler [R] — *P. trochiloides*
One or two birds are seen annually at Locke Park, Hartlepool headland and Spurn.

Arctic warbler [R] — *P. borealis*
One at Flamborough in '83.

Radde's warbler [R] — *P. schwarzi*
Another rare warbler, one or two seen at Spurn in autumn '87 and '88.

Dusky warbler [R] — *P. puscatus*
One in the mid '70's at South Landing Flamborough and another in '85.

Bonelli's warbler [R] — *P. bonelli*
One reported from an orchard in Holme on Spalding Moor in '83.

Wood warbler — *P. sibilatrix*
Breeds in woodland in the east of the county, but absent from the Wolds. Single birds seen on passage in autumn.

Chiffchaff — *P. collybita*
Frequent in all mature woods [Common Chiffchaff].

Willow warbler — *P. trochilus*
Seen in gardens, scrub, woods, and hedges everywhere.

Goldcrest — *Regulus regulus*
One of our smallest birds, breeding in coniferous woods; large numbers move along the coast in autumn after easterly winds.

Firecrest — *R. ignicapillus*
Much brighter than goldcrest, and much less common. Single birds are reported from Spurn and Flamborough each autumn.

Spotted flycatcher — *Muscicapa striata*
Frequently encountered on the edges of woods or in parks and gardens in summer.

Spotted flycatcher.

Red-breasted flycatcher — *Fidecula parva*
Seen on passage each year in autumn with single birds at places such as Scarborough or Filey.

Pied flycatcher — *F. hypoleuca*
Breeds along rivers in the Dales, and seen frequently in trees and scrub along the coast in autumn.

Collared flycatcher [R] — *F. albicollis*
A bird of central Europe, but one was at Filey in the spring of '85.

Bearded reedling — *Panurus biarmicus*
Blacktoft Sands is the best place to see these birds, especially in autumn when they collect in large feeding parties. They breed in several localities along the Humber [Bearded Parrotbill].

Penduline tit [R] — *Remiz pendulinus*
A potential coloniser of this country, and a pair were seen at the turn of the year in 81/82 at Blacktoft Sands during a period of intense cold. They survived into the New Year, but presumably either died or moved on. Another pair turned up briefly in autumn '88 [Masked Penduline-tit].

Long-tailed tit — *Aegithalos caudatus*
Breeds in woodland around the county, and moves in family parties in autumn [Long-tailed Bush-tit].

Marsh tit — *Parus palustris*
Common in woodland in the Wolds, and in Forge valley, but restricted to mature plantations.

Willow tit — *P. montanus*
Seen throughout the area, wherever there is scrub. Often visits garden bird tables in winter.

Coal tit — *P. ater*
A species that has benefited from coniferous woodlands. They often are seen in Leylandii cyprusses in towns.

Blue tit — *P. caeruleus*
A familiar and popular acrobat that frequents clothes lines, milk bottles, and breeds successfully in home made nest boxes.

Great tit — *P. major*
Not as common as the last species, but just as widely distributed.

Nuthatch — *Sitta europaea*
Remarkably scarce in many areas with only a few wintering records from Teesside, one breeding site in Humberside, but several pairs at Forge Valley.

Treecreeper — *Certhia familiaris*
Widespread with many breeding pairs in the area, and there is a small influx of continental birds each autumn.

Golden oriole — *Oriolus oriolus*
A beautiful bird that breeds in East Anglia, and each year isolated individuals turn up at Spurn or Flamborough.

Red-backed shrike — Lanius collurio
Mainly observed as juveniles in the autumn when several birds are seen each year on the coast.

Isabelline shrike [R] — *L. isabellinus*
A young bird stayed for a week, and was well watched at Spurn in '88.

Lesser grey shrike [R] — *L. minor*
One at Flamborough in '82 and a long stayer at Spurn in '81.

Great grey shrike — *L. excubitor*
Seen occasionally along the Lower Derwent in winter, and single birds are seen regularly along the coast each year.

Woodchat shrike [R] — *L. senator*
One at Holmpton near Withernsea in '83, and another at Bempton in '86.

Jay — Garrulus glandarius
A noisy woodland bird that is found all over the east. Occasionally

large concentrations of birds come in from the continent in October [Acorn Jay].

Magpie — *Pica pica*
A common bird in all towns and urban areas, but much lower numbers are found in the Wolds [Black-billed Magpie].

Jackdaw — *Corvus monedula*
Feeds with large flocks of rooks in arable fields everywhere [Western Jackdaw].

Rook — *C. frugilegus*
Roosts of up to 10,000 have been recorded in some areas; a communal bird that has suffered a bad press due to its similarity to the next species.

Carrion crow — *C. corone*
Despite some of their habits they do a useful job in the countryside by removing dead animals. Hooded crows are often seen on the coast in winter.

Raven — *C. corax*
The largest passerine. Very rare in the east, but there have been breeding records from the north west of Yorkshire in recent years [Common Raven].

Starling — *Sturnus vulgaris*
Roosts in huge flocks in cities, which creates quite a problem for those passing beneath their roosts! Despite being noisy, and quarrelsome they are very attractive birds [Common Starling].

Rose-coloured starling [R] — *S. roseus*
One at Flamborough in '84 was an adult, but most records from the past usually refer to juveniles.

House sparrow — *Passer domesticus*
A familiar garden bird that collects in post breeding flocks and feeds on grain in arable fields.

Tree sparrow — *P. montanus*
Breeds in many woodlands and small flocks are often seen on the coast in winter [Eurasian Tree Sparrow].

Chaffinch — *Fringilla coelebs*
Common in all parks and woodlands [Common Chaffinch].

Brambling — *F. montifringilla*
A winter visitor, arriving on the coast in small flocks from October onwards. They can often be seen feeding under beech trees.

Serin [R] — *Serinus serinus*
One at Locke Park in '85 and '86 [European Serin].

Greenfinch — *Carduelis chloris*
Breeds in gardens and woodlands throughout the area [Western Greenfinch].

Goldfinch — *C. carduelis*
A pretty finch that can often be seen feeding on thistles [Common Goldfinch].

Siskin — *C. spinus*
There are isolated breeding records throughout the county, but the numbers are swollen each winter by large flocks of immigrant birds [Spruce Siskin].

Linnet — *Acanthis cannabina*
Fond of gorse and broom. Found all over the area, they form small flocks in autumn [Brown Linnet].

Twite — *C. flavirostris*
Twite breed on moorland areas in the West Riding, and many move to the coast in winter.

Redpoll — *Z. flammea*
Partial to silver birch seeds, and can be found wherever there are birch plantations. The continental race 'mealy redpoll' occurs with flocks of redpoll in winter [Common Redpoll].

Arctic redpoll [R] — *Z. hornemanni*
One or two records from the coast in recent years, and one at York University in '85.

Crossbill — *Loxia curvirostra*
Pairs breed at Dalby forest, and probably Allerthorpe Common, as juvenile birds are seem from time to time [Common Crossbill].

Parrot crossbill [R] — *L. pytyopsittacus*
The first recorded breeding of this species in the country was in the south of Yorkshire in '83. Occasionally seen at the coast.

Scarlet rosefinch — *Carpodacus erythrinus*
Occurs at Spurn and Flamborough most years; a female was at South Gare in May '87.

Bullfinch — *Pyrrhula pyrrhula*
Widely distributed, especially where there are fruit trees, as they are partial to the young buds, and can reduce yields in commercial plantations [Northern Bullfinch].

Hawfinch — *Coccothraustes coccothraustes*
Common only in the Scrayingham area near York, and at Mature woodland in Guisborough. Very timid at times and best seen in the early months of the year.

White-throated sparrow [R] — *Z. leucophrys*
One ringed at Spurn in '83 was the first Yorkshire record.

White-crowned sparrow
Another American passerine, one at Hornsea Mere in Spring '77.

Lapland bunting — *Calcarius lapponicus*
Seen every winter along Bridlington Bay with Barmston being the easiest place to see them.

Snow bunting — *Plectrophenax nivalis*
A flock of snow buntings rising from a snowy stubble field on a bleak January morning makes the early rise worth it all! These icy birds

congregate each winter from North Gare to Spurn in groups often over 100 strong.

Yellowhammer — *Emberiza citrinella*
A common hedgerow bird all over the area.

Cirl Bunting — *Emberiza cirllus*
A female near Tophill Low in '85.

Ortolan bunting — *E. hortulana*
Single birds are recorded most years from well watched points along the coast.

Rustic bunting [R] — *E. rustica*
One at Filey Dams in spring '85.

Yellow-breasted bunting — *E. aureola*
Another rare bunting. A young bird was at Flamborough in '82.

Little bunting [R] — *E. pusilla*
The most recent was at South Gare in autumn '88.

Reed bunting — *E. schoeniclus*
Common at all reedbeds, and marshy areas.

Corn bunting — *E. calandra*
In spring they are conspicuous as they deliver their jangling song from telephone wires and fences; in autumn large flocks can be found in open fields.

Swifts around a church steeple.

CLUBS AND SOCIETIES

It is very useful for novice and experienced birdwatchers alike to be able to meet other people with similar interests. The following list of clubs and societies should help provide the opportunity to share experiences and improve one's knowledge of birds by meeting others with greater experience. The details may change from year to year, but a general idea of the kinds of activities is provided.

York RSPB group
Contact — Membership secretary, Mrs J. Caldwell, Counters Gate, Church Lane, Moor Monkton, York.
Activities — Indoor meetings are held monthly from September to April at Temple Hall, College of St. John, Lord Mayor's Walk, York.
    Talks are given by RSPB staff, local and national ornithological personalities, on wide ranging topics from home and abroad, illustrated by slides.
    There are monthly coach outings to reserves such as Martin Mere, Holy Island, Gouthwaite reservoir and Filey Brigg. Once a year there is a National film show at York University where the latest RSPB films can be seen.
    A newsletter is sent out to members three times a year.

York Young Ornithologists' Club.
Contact — York City library for up to date details of current activities.
Group leader — Rhona Lowe (Tel: York 798100).
Activities — All meetings are outdoor and cover many aspects of nature study.
    Groups are kept to 6-8 children per group and there are about 12 group leaders. Visits are made to a variety of habitats over the year including local nature reserves, the North York Moors, Blacktoft Sands etc.
    The club is thriving and places a strong emphasis on conservation of the environment.

York Birdwatchers' Club
Contact — Ian Newton (Tel: York 53151).
Activities — This group meets at Priory Street Community Centre on the first Tuesday of each month except for July and August.

Indoor meetings include talks, quiz nights, slide shows etc. and there is a trip organised each month to the coast, the moors, or to a reserve. The club members tend to be of the more experienced kind of bird enthusiast, but beginners would learn a lot from being a member. The club does a lot of recording of bird numbers, and produces an annual report covering the Vale of York south to the Humber.

Bridlington RSPB
Contact — Paul Leyland (Tel: Scarborough 891507).
Activities — Indoor meetings are held at Bridlington Library on the 3rd or 4th Tuesday in the month from September to April.

Talks are mainly on birds, but other aspects of wildlife such as butterflies and mammals are also covered. There are field trips every month except for August.

Filey Brigg Ornithological Group
This is a group of local birdwatchers who are active recording and ringing birds, and welcome records from other local people and visitors to the area. They produce an annual report which can be obtained from the café on North Cliff Country Park, or from the recorder — Peter Dunn (Tel: Scarborough 583149).

Scarborough Birdwatchers' Club
There are a lot of birdwatchers in this area, and they meet regularly, but informally at the Turk's Head, Eastborough on the 3rd Thursday of each month. They have guest speakers most meetings but are just as likely to chat about local birds over a pint or two.

Beverley Naturalists' Society
Contact — Mervin Nethercoat, 44 Thurston Road, Beverley.
Activities — Indoor meetings are held in the Minster Parish Rooms on Mondays throughout the year.

Outdoor activities are held on Sundays and include visits to the estuary for wader counts, walks along Pocklington Canal, Millington Woods, and Gibralter Point. The group has also had 'bird races' to see which group can see the most species in a day.

Scarborough Field Naturalists' Society
Contact — Tel: Scarborough 361806 for details or from the notice board in the library at Vernon Road.

Meetings are held fortnightly on Tuesday evenings at 7.30 at the library, and topics such as birds, fungi, butterflies, mammals, flowers, etc. are covered. New members are welcome!

Hull and District Ornithological Group
Contact — Andy Gibson (Tel: Hull 65855).
Activities — The group meets informally every Thursday evening at The Royal Standard in Beverley, and meets formally on the 2nd Wednesday of each month, with the exception of December, at the Y.P.I. George St. Hull.

The group holds very friendly and relaxed meetings, and covers all aspects of wildlife as well as birds. Most indoor meetings are talks, which are always illustrated with slides. There are field trips each month, and 2 or 3 times a year there are coach outings to reserves or sites of special interest.

Full details are published in their programme.

Hull RSPB
Contact — Dick Parret (Tel: Hull 811380).
Activities — All indoor meetings are held at the Church Memorial Hall, Kirkella, at 7.30 on the 1st Tuesday of each month from September to July.

Most of the talks are on birds, but other aspects of wildlife also get covered in their programme. There are outdoor trips arranged each month to places such as Clumber Park, Spurn, Brough Haven, Martin Mere etc.

Hull YOC
Contact — Martin Hollingsworth (Tel: Hull 446378).
Activities — The group works very closely alongside the Hull RSPB members' group. Details of meetings and outings can be obtained from either the above contact or the RSPB group.

Teesmouth Bird Club
Contact — John Dunnett (Tel: Middlesbrough 595845).
Activities — This group is exclusively devoted to the study of birds, and meets formally on the 1st Wednesday of each month from

September to April at the Billingham Arms Hotel, and meets informally on the 2nd Wednesday of each month at the Municipal Golf Club. As well as the evening meetings there are 4 or 5 excursions each year to various places around the estuary, and 2 trips to the Farne Islands.

Cleveland RSPB
Contact — Chris Brown (Tel: Middlesbrough 822397).
Activities — Meets September to April at Leeds University Centre, Harrow Road on the 1st Monday of each month.

Although principally interested in birds, the group has talks on other aspects of wildlife such as flowers. As well as the evening meetings there are 4 coach trips each year.

Cleveland East YOC
Contact — Lin Treadgold (Tel: Guisborough 76579).

This is a very lively group with lots of children involved in many aspects of nature study; in fact some of them have recently been on T.V. with BBC TV from Bempton. The group needs more leaders, so if you enjoy birds AND helping children, then they want to hear from you! Most of the meetings are outdoor.

Whitby RSPB
Contact — Denis Welford (Tel: Whitby 840202).
Activities — The club is open to non-RSPB members as well as members, and meets at Caedman School on every 4th Wednesday from September to April. Outdoor events include trips to local sites of interest.

Young Ornithologists' Club
The Lodge, Sandy, Bedfordshire.

This is the junior branch of RSPB and encourages young people to take an interest in conservation through bird study. They have a summer migrants hot-line for reporting early arrivals, and local groups put up nest boxes as well as undertaking many other important and interesting projects. *Bird Study* is sent free to all members.

NATIONAL AND REGIONAL SOCIETIES

Royal Society for the Protection of Birds
The Lodge, Sandy, Bedfordshire.

Every birdwatcher, and all people interested in nature study and conservation should belong to this organisation. They are responsible for the maintenance and protection of thousands of acres of fragile countryside throughout the British Isles, including Blacktoft Sands, Hornsea Mere, and Bempton Cliffs in our own area.

Their magazine *Birds* is sent free to all members every quarter, which at the time of writing stands at 440,000.

Young Ornithologists' Club
The Lodge, Sandy, Bedfordshire.

This is the junior branch of RSPB and encourages young people to take an interest in conservation through bird study. They have a summer migrants hot-line for reporting early arrivals, and local groups put up nest boxes as well as undertaking many other important and interesting projects. *Bird Study* is sent free to all members.

British Trust for Ornithology
Beech Grove, Tring, Herts.

The BTO involves local birdwatchers in scientific studies of population changes, and migration patterns of birds. They conduct a census each year of the nesting distribution of common birds, and organise ringing courses each year for permit holders. The results of these studies are published in *Bird Study* which comes out 3 times a year.

Yorkshire Wildlife Trust
10 Toft Gdn., York (Tel: 659570).

Nearly 50 reserves are managed throughout the county of Yorkshire. Some of these are of national importance such as Spurn Point and Grass Woods, whilst others are small reserves protecting local habitats that otherwise could fall to the plough or the "developer". All these sites cost hard cash to maintain, and their resources are always stretched, so support them by joining if you can. A wallet containing up to date details of all of the 50 reserves can be purchased from the above address. This will give you a complete picture of each reserve.

Cleveland Nature Conservation Trust
Old Town Hall, Mandale Road, Thornaby, TS17 6AW.

Details of membership can be obtained from this address. They are affiliated to the Royal Society for Nature Conservation, and send out regular newsletters, together with details of activities in the area of conservation in Cleveland. They have recently produced a broadsheet called *Greenbits* which reports current issues, such as industrial threats to remaining habitat, school nature study and urban wildlife sanctuaries.

Lincolnshire and South Humberside Conservation Trust

Most of their reserves are outside our area such as at Gibraltar Point, but Far Ings at Barton on Humber is managed by them, and if you are interested in membership, then details may be obtained from their office at Lincoln.

Kingfisher.

FURTHER READING

County reports for Cleveland and Yorkshire
Cleveland Trust for Nature Conservation
Yorkshire Wildlife Trust
Spurn Bird Reports
British Birds annual report on rare birds in Britain
Humberside County Council

SOURCES OF INFORMATION

In addition to the annual County reports, the following periodicals will be of value to the birdwatcher who wants to increase his or her knowledge of birds:

British Birds
This is a monthly magazine that any one who calls his or herself a birdwatcher should subscribe to. It has excellent photography in it, and contains papers on the identification of difficult species, breeding biology of birds, mystery photographs, recent reports, and readers' notes. It can only be obtained from British Birds, Fountains, Park Lane, Blunham, Bedfordshire.

Birdwatching
This is a new magazine that is more chatty than British Birds, and can be obtained from any newsagent upon request. It has articles on reserves, migration, conservation, birding trips, and there is a regional round up of latest records compiled by their own local contacts. It is an ideal periodical for any one who is getting started in birdwatching, and for any one who wants to keep up to date with national events.

Birding World
This is a relatively new magazine which has rapidly acquired a good reputation for keeping readers up to date with recent sightings. It is obtained by subscription and this also provides readers with a hot line telephone number to find out what rare birds have been seen each day. The journal contains papers on identification of tricky species, reviews of new books, etc. Subscription details can be obtained from 'Stonerunner', Coast Road, Cley-next-the-Sea, Norfolk.

CHECK LIST

This is a list of all the birds that may be seen in the area. You can use it to keep a check on the ones that you have seen.

[ ] Red-throated diver
[ ] Black-throated diver
[ ] Great northern diver
[ ] White-billed diver
[ ] Pied-billed grebe
[ ] Little grebe
[ ] Black-necked grebe
[ ] Slavonian grebe
[ ] Red-necked grebe
[ ] Great crested grebe
[ ] Black-browed albatross
[ ] Fulmar
[ ] Capped petrel
[ ] Cory's shearwater
[ ] Great shearwater
[ ] Sooty shearwater
[ ] Manx shearwater
[ ] Ballearic shearwater
[ ] Little shearwater
[ ] Storm petrel
[ ] Leach's petrel
[ ] Gannet
[ ] Cormorant
[ ] Double crested Cormorant
[ ] Shag
[ ] Bittern
[ ] Little bittern
[ ] Night heron
[ ] Green heron
[ ] Cattle egret
[ ] Great white egret
[ ] Little egret
[ ] Grey heron
[ ] Purple heron
[ ] White stork
[ ] Spoonbill
[ ] Canada goose
[ ] Barnacle goose
[ ] Brent goose
[ ] Red-breasted goose
[ ] Greylag goose
[ ] White-fronted goose
[ ] Lesser white-fronted goose
[ ] Bean goose
[ ] Pink-footed goose
[ ] Snow goose
[ ] Mute swan

[ ] Whooper swan
[ ] Bewick's swan
[ ] Ruddy shelduck
[ ] Shelduck
[ ] Egyptian goose
[ ] Mallard
[ ] Black duck
[ ] Teal
[ ] Gadwall
[ ] Wigeon
[ ] American wigeon
[ ] Pintail
[ ] Garganey
[ ] Blue-winged teal
[ ] Shoveller
[ ] Pochard
[ ] Red-crested pochard
[ ] Ring-necked duck
[ ] Ferruginous duck
[ ] Tufted duck
[ ] Scaup
[ ] Mandarin
[ ] Eider
[ ] Common scoter
[ ] Velvet scoter
[ ] Surf scoter
[ ] Long-tailed duck
[ ] Goldeneye
[ ] Smew
[ ] Red-brested merganser
[ ] Goosander
[ ] Ruddy duck
[ ] Osprey
[ ] Honey buzzard
[ ] Red kite
[ ] Black kite
[ ] White-tailed eagle
[ ] Goshawk

[ ] Sparrowhawk
[ ] Rough-legged buzzard
[ ] Buzzard
[ ] Golden eagle
[ ] Hen harrier
[ ] Montagu's harrier
[ ] Marsh harrier
[ ] Gyr falcon

[ ] Peregrine
[ ] Hobby
[ ] Eleonora's falcon
[ ] Merlin
[ ] Red-footed falcon
[ ] Lesser kestrel
[ ] Kestrel
[ ] Red grouse
[ ] Red-legged partridge
[ ] Grey partridge
[ ] Quail
[ ] Pheasant
[ ] Crane
[ ] Water rail
[ ] Spotted crake
[ ] Corncrake
[ ] Moorhen
[ ] Coot
[ ] Oystercatcher
[ ] Ringed plover
[ ] Little ringed plover
[ ] Kentish plover
[ ] Greater sand plover
[ ] Dotterel
[ ] Golden plover
[ ] American golden plover
[ ] Pacific golden plover
[ ] Grey plover
[ ] Lapwing
[ ] Turnstone
[ ] Semipalmated sandpiper
[ ] Little stint
[ ] Temminck's stint
[ ] Long-toed stint
[ ] Red-necked stint
[ ] White-rumped sandpiper
[ ] Baird's sandpiper
[ ] Pectoral sandpiper
[ ] Sharp-tailed sandpiper
[ ] Purple sandpiper
[ ] Dunlin
[ ] Curlew sandpiper
[ ] Knot
[ ] Sanderling
[ ] Ruff
[ ] Buff-breasted sandpiper
[ ] Broad-billed sandpiper
[ ] Long-billed dowitcher
[ ] Spotted redshank
[ ] Redshank
[ ] Marsh sandpiper
[ ] Greenshank
[ ] Lesser yellowlegs

[ ] Green sandpiper
[ ] Wood sandpiper
[ ] Common sandpiper
[ ] Spotted sandpiper
[ ] Black-tailed godwit
[ ] Bar-tailed godwit
[ ] Hudsonian godwit
[ ] Curlew
[ ] Whimbrel
[ ] Woodcock
[ ] Snipe
[ ] Jack snipe
[ ] Black-winged stilt
[ ] Avocet
[ ] Grey phalarope
[ ] Red-necked phalarope
[ ] Wilson's phalarope
[ ] Collared pratincole
[ ] Great skua
[ ] Pomarine skua
[ ] Arctic skua
[ ] Long-tailed skua
[ ] Mediterranean gull
[ ] Laughing gull
[ ] Little gull
[ ] Sabine's gull
[ ] Bonaparte's gull
[ ] Black-headed gull
[ ] Lesser black-backed gull

[ ] Greater black-backed gull
[ ] Herring gull
[ ] Iceland gull
[ ] Glaucous gull
[ ] Common gull
[ ] Ring-billed gull
[ ] Kittiwake
[ ] Ross's gull
[ ] Ivory gull
[ ] Black tern
[ ] White-winged black tern
[ ] Caspian tern
[ ] Lesser crested tern
[ ] Sandwich tern
[ ] Common tern
[ ] Arctic tern
[ ] Roseate tern
[ ] Little tern
[ ] Little auk
[ ] Razorbill
[ ] Guillemot
[ ] Black guillemot
[ ] Puffin

[ ] Woodpigeon
[ ] Stock dove
[ ] Rock dove
[ ] Collared dove
[ ] Turtle dove
[ ] Cuckoo
[ ] Yellow-billed cuckoo
[ ] Great spotted cuckoo
[ ] Barn owl
[ ] Long-eared owl
[ ] Short-eared owl
[ ] Little owl
[ ] Tengmalm's owl
[ ] Tawny owl
[ ] Nightjar
[ ] Swift
[ ] Alpine swift
[ ] Kingfisher
[ ] Bee-eater
[ ] Hoopoe
[ ] Wryneck
[ ] Green woodpecker
[ ] Great spotted woodpecker
[ ] Lesser spotted woodpecker
[ ] Short-toed lark
[ ] Shore lark
[ ] Woodlark
[ ] Skylark
[ ] Sand martin
[ ] Swallow
[ ] Red-rumped swallow
[ ] House martin
[ ] Richard's pipit
[ ] Tawny pipit
[ ] Tree pipit
[ ] Olive-backed pipit
[ ] Pechora pipit
[ ] Meadow pipit
[ ] Red-throated pipit
[ ] Rock pipit
[ ] Water pipit
[ ] Yellow wagtail
[ ] Grey wagtail
[ ] Pied wagtail
[ ] Red-backed shrike
[ ] Woodchat shrike
[ ] Isabelline shrike
[ ] Lesser grey shrike
[ ] Great grey shrike
[ ] Waxwing
[ ] Dipper
[ ] Wren
[ ] Dunnock

[ ] Cetti's warbler
[ ] Savi's warbler
[ ] River warbler
[ ] Grasshopper warbler
[ ] Aquatic warbler
[ ] Sedge warbler
[ ] Paddyfield warbler
[ ] Blyth's reed warbler
[ ] Marsh warbler
[ ] Reed warbler
[ ] Great reed warbler
[ ] Icterine warbler
[ ] Melodious warbler
[ ] Booted warbler
[ ] Barred warbler
[ ] Garden warbler
[ ] Blackcap
[ ] Whitethroat
[ ] Lesser whitethroat
[ ] Sardinian warbler
[ ] Subalpine warbler
[ ] Willow warbler
[ ] Chiffchaff
[ ] Bonelli's warbler
[ ] Wood warbler
[ ] Dusky warbler
[ ] Radde's warbler
[ ] Yellow-browed warbler
[ ] Pallas's warbler
[ ] Greenish warbler
[ ] Arctic warbler
[ ] Goldcrest
[ ] Firecrest
[ ] Pied flycatcher
[ ] Collared flycatcher
[ ] Red-breasted flycatcher
[ ] Spotted flycatcher
[ ] Whinchat
[ ] Stonechat
[ ] Wheatear
[ ] Rock thrush
[ ] Black redstart
[ ] Redstart
[ ] Robin
[ ] Nightingale
[ ] Thrush nightingale
[ ] Bluethroat
[ ] Fieldfare
[ ] Ring ouzel
[ ] Blackbird
[ ] Redwing
[ ] Song thrush
[ ] Mistle thrush

- [ ] Bearded reedling
- [ ] Long-tailed tit
- [ ] Marsh tit
- [ ] Willow tit
- [ ] Coal tit
- [ ] Blue tit
- [ ] Great tit
- [ ] Penduline tit
- [ ] Nuthatch
- [ ] Treecreeper
- [ ] Corn bunting
- [ ] Yellowhammer
- [ ] Ortolan bunting
- [ ] Little bunting
- [ ] Rustic bunting
- [ ] Reed bunting
- [ ] Lapland bunting
- [ ] Snow bunting
- [ ] White-throated sparrow
- [ ] Chaffinch
- [ ] Brambling
- [ ] Serin
- [ ] Greenfinch
- [ ] Twite
- [ ] Linnet
- [ ] Siskin
- [ ] Goldfinch
- [ ] Redpoll
- [ ] Arctic redpoll
- [ ] Scarlet rosefinch
- [ ] Parrot crossbill
- [ ] Crossbill
- [ ] Bullfinch
- [ ] Hawfinch
- [ ] House sparrow
- [ ] Tree sparrow
- [ ] Starling
- [ ] Golden oriole
- [ ] Jay
- [ ] Magpie
- [ ] Jackdaw
- [ ] Rook
- [ ] Carrion crow
- [ ] Raven

ALPHABETICAL INDEX

(Entries refer to Species List only)

Albatross, black-browed 67
Auk, little 88
Avocet 79

Bee-eater 91
Bittern 69
    little 69
Blackbird 95
Blackcap 98
Bluethroat 94
Brambling 103
Bullfinch 104
Bunting, cirl 105
    corn 105
    Lapland 104
    little 105
    ortolan 105
    reed 105
    rustic 105
    snow 104
    yellow-breasted 105
Buzzard 76
    honey 75
    rough-legged 76

Chaffinch 103
Chiffchaff 99
Coot 79
Cormorant 69
    double-crested 69
Corncrake 79
Crake, spotted 78
Crane 79
Crossbill 104
    parrot 104
Crow 102
Cuckoo 89
    great spotted 89
    yellow-billed 89
Curlew 83
    stone 80

Dipper 94
Diver, black-throated 66
    great northern 66
    red-throated 66
    white-billed 66

Dotterel 80
Dove, collared 89
    rock 89
    stock 89
    turtle 89
Dowitcher, long-billed 83
Duck,
    long-tailed 74
    ring-necked 73
    ruddy 75
    tufted 73
Dunlin 82
Dunnock 94

Eagle, golden 76
    white-tailed 75
Egret, cattle 69
    great white 70
    little 70
Eider 74

Falcon, Eleonora's 77
    gyr 77
    peregrine 78
    red-footed 76
Fieldfare 95
Firecrest 99
Flycatcher, collared 100
    pied 100
    red-breasted 100
    spotted 99
Fulmar 67

Gadwall 73
Gannet 68
Garganey 73
Godwit, bar-tailed 83
    black-tailed 83
    Hudsonian 83
Goldcrest 99
Goldeneye 74
    Barrow's 74
Goldfinch 103
Goosander 75
Goose, barnacle 72
    bean 71
    Brent 72

Canada 72
Egyptian 72
greylag 71
lesser white-fronted............. 71
pink-footed 71
red-breasted 72
snow 71
white-fronted 71
Goshawk............................ 76
Grebe, black-necked................ 67
great crested.................... 67
little 66
red-necked 67
Slavonian 67
Greenfinch......................... 103
Greenshank......................... 84
Grouse, red........................ 78
Guillemot.......................... 88
black 88
Gull, black-headed 86
Bonaparte's...................... 86
common 86
glaucous 87
great black-backed 87
herring 86
Iceland 87
ivory............................ 87
laughing 86
lesser black-backed.............. 86
little 86
Mediterranean 86
ring-billed gull 86
Ross's 87
Sabine's 86

Harrier, hen 75
marsh 75
Montagu's 75
Hawfinch 104
Heron, green-backed 69
grey............................. 70
purple........................... 70
squacco 70
Hobby.............................. 77
Hoopoe 91

Jackdaw 102
Jay................................ 101

Kestrel............................ 76
lesser 76
Kingfisher......................... 91
Kite, black........................ 75

red............................... 75
Kittiwake 87
Knot............................... 81

Lapwing 81
Lark, shore........................ 92
short-toed....................... 91
sky.............................. 92
wood............................. 92
Linnet............................. 103

Magpie............................. 102
Mallard 73
Martin, house 92
sand............................. 92
Merganser, red-breasted 74
Merlin............................. 77
Moorhen............................ 79

Nightingale 94
thrush........................... 94
Nightjar........................... 91
Nuthatch........................... 101

Oriole, golden..................... 101
Osprey 76
Ouzel, ring........................ 95
Owl, barn.......................... 89
little 90
long-eared 90
short-eared 90
tawny 90
Tengmalm's 90
Oystercatcher...................... 79

Partridge, grey 78
red-legged....................... 78
Petrel, capped 67
Leech's.......................... 68
storm............................ 68
Phalarope, grey 85
red-necked....................... 85
Wilson's 85
Pheasant 78
Pintail 72
Pipit, meadow...................... 93
olive-backed..................... 93
red-throated..................... 93
Richard's 92
rock 93
tawny 92
tree 93
water 93

Plover, American golden 80
    golden............................ 80
    greater sand 80
    grey.............................. 80
    Kentish........................... 80
    little ringed 80
    Pacific golden 80
    ringed 80
Pochard............................... 73
Pratincole, collared 79
Puffin................................ 89

Quail 78

Rail, water........................... 78
Raven 102
Razorbill............................. 88
Redpoll............................... 103
    Arctic 104
    mealy............................ 103
Redshank 84
    spotted........................... 84
Redstart.............................. 95
    black 95
Redwing 96
Reedling, bearded.................... 100
Robin................................. 94
Rook 102
Rosefinch, scarlet 104
Ruff.................................. 82

Sanderling 81
Sandpiper, Baird's 82
    broad-billed 82
    buff-breasted 82
    common 85
    curlew........................... 82
    green 84
    pectoral 82
    purple........................... 82
    semi-palmated.................... 81
    sharp-tailed..................... 82
    spotted.......................... 85
    white-rumped 82
    wood 85
Scaup................................. 74
Scoter, common 74
    surf............................. 74
    velvet........................... 74
Serin................................. 103
Shag 69
Shearwater, Balearic................. 68
    Cory's........................... 67

    great............................ 68
    little 68
    Manx............................. 68
    sooty 68
Shelduck 72
    ruddy............................ 72
Shoveller............................. 73
Shrike great grey.................... 101
    Isabelline....................... 101
    lesser grey 101
    red-backed....................... 101
    woodchat......................... 101
Siskin................................ 103
Skua, Arctic.......................... 85
    great............................ 85
    long-tailed 85
    Pomarine 85
Smew.................................. 74
Snipe 83
    great............................ 83
    jack............................. 83
Sparrow, house 102
    tree............................. 103
    white-crowned 104
    white-throated 104
Sparrowhawk 76
Spoonbill............................. 70
Starling.............................. 102
    rose-coloured.................... 102
Stilt, black-winged.................. 79
Stint, little 81
    long-toed 81
    red-necked....................... 81
    Temminck's 81
Stonechat 95
Stork, white 70
Swallow............................... 92
    red-rumped....................... 92
Swan, Bewick's....................... 71
    mute............................. 70
    whooper 71
Swift................................. 91
    Alpine........................... 91

Teal.................................. 72
    blue-winged 73
Tern, Arctic.......................... 88
    black 88
    Caspian.......................... 87
    common 88
    gull-billed...................... 87
    little 88
    roseate 87

Sandwich 87
whiskered 88
white-winged black 88
Thrush, eye-browed 95
mistle 96
rock 95
song 96
Tit, blue 101
coal 100
great 101
long-tailed 100
marsh 100
penduline 100
willow 100
Treecreeper 101
Turnstone 81
Twite 103

Wagtail, grey 93
pied 94
yellow 93
Warbler, aquatic 96
Arctic 98
barred 97
Blyth's reed 96
Bonelli's 98
booted 97
Cetti's 96
desert 97
dusky 98
garden 98
grasshopper 96
great reed 97

greenish 98
icterine 97
marsh 97
melodious 97
Pallas's 98
Radde's 98
reed 97
river 96
Sardinian 97
Savi's 96
sedge 96
subalpine 97
willow 99
wood 98
yellow-browed 98
Waxwing 94
Wheatear 95
Whimbrel 83
Whinchat 95
Whitethroat 98
lesser 97
Wigeon 72
Woodcock 83
Woodpecker, Great spotted 91
green 91
lesser spotted 91
Woodpigeon 89
Wren 94
Wryneck 91

Yellowhammer 105
Yellowlegs, lesser 84

Great tit.

120